SAINTS

for
Young People
for Every Day
of the Year

Vol. I (Jan. — June)

BY THE DAUGHTERS OF ST. PAUL

ST. PAUL EDITIONS

IMPRIMATUR:
✠Richard Cardinal Cushing

Volume I
ISBN 0-8198-0143-7 c
    0-8198-0144-5 p

Library of Congress Catalog Card Number: 63-19997

Printed in the U.S.A. by the Daughters of St. Paul
50 St. Paul's Ave., Boston, MA 02130

The Daughters of St. Paul are an international congregation of
women religious serving the Church with the communications media.

I will make a little progress in virtue every day until death.

DEDICATED TO

THE SERVANT OF GOD

Maggiorino Vigolungo

A teenager of our times who reached a hero's level of love for God and man by following his challenging slogan:
"Make a little progress every day."

Known as the young apostle of the press, this manly boy, at the age of twelve, joined the newly founded Society of St. Paul in his native Italy and his burning ideals shine clearly in these declarations of his: *"With the help of God, I intend and resolve to consecrate my entire life to spreading the Message of Christ through the Apostolate of the Press." "I want to become a saint, a great saint—and soon!" "Pray for me that I may not betray my vocation which is the best of all!"*

God willed to call Maggiorino when he was only fourteen, but he was ready. He had written: *"Heaven! Eternal happiness! This is what is waiting for me!"*

5

Dear Reader:

In "Saints for Young People for Every Day of the Year", you are going to enjoy stories and examples about a great many different Saints—three hundred and sixty-five, in fact. You will find that some lived long lives, while others died when they were very young. You will discover that some gave themselves completely to God in their childhood or teens, while others learned the hard way that only He can make us happy. You will see pictures of saints who were beautiful and fair, Saints who were wrinkled from age, Saints who were strong and valiant, and Saints who were weak and sickly.

You will be surprised by the differences in their names. Some you will easily recognize, but at others you may lift up your eyebrows—Alphege, for example, or Cunegundes.

You will meet people from every nation and race, and from many different centuries, starting with the early days of the Church and coming right down to our own times.

You will come to know saintly kings and peasants, queens and housemaids, popes and priests, sisters and brothers, doctors and farmers, soldiers and lawyers, mothers and fathers, young men and women, and boys and girls!

Yes, the Saints came from all walks of life. How did they all reach sanctity? Were they born saints? Oh, no! They were made of flesh and blood, as we are. And they lived on this earth, suffered temptations and faced problems. But they became saints because they used their will power and prayed. They corrected their defects and did God's Will as well as they possibly could.

All the Saints were alike in one way: they loved God very much. But they were all different because God's Will was different for each one of them and because they all showed their love for God in different ways. Yet every one of them is a great hero, a brilliant star who fought for and won eternal fame and glory.

What is the best way to read these lives of the Saints? Well, first of all, do not try to read all three hundred and sixty-five Saints in only five days. Just read one Saint a day. But, you say, it will take a whole year then! And you are right. That is the way to do it. Keep these true stories by your bedside and read the Saint of the day before or after your morning or evening prayers. In this way, you will be able to think about what you read now and again during the day. Then, if you make the resolution you will find after each story, slowly but surely you will see an improvement in yourself. And there is no telling where you may go from there. Maybe you, too, will become a Saint! And why not?

Here is a friendly tip: if you find it hard to keep your resolution, why not ask the Saint of the day to help you? By the end of the year you will have three hundred and sixty-five heavenly helpers!

Contents for Volume One

JANUARY

FEBRUARY

MARCH

10

APRIL

MAY

JUNE

~~

JANUARY 1

The Circumcision of Our Lord

On the eighth day after His birth, Jesus was brought to the temple by Mary and Joseph to be circumcised. Circumcision was a painful religious ceremony performed on Jewish boys eight days after they were born. On that day they also received their name, and they became members of God's Chosen People. St. Luke tells us: "And after eight days were accomplished, that the Child should be circumcised, His name was called Jesus, which was called by the Angel, before He was conceived in the womb." The holy name of Jesus means "Savior," and it is the sweetest and most powerful name.

Mary was not bound to bring Jesus to the temple, but out of her great love and respect for the Law of Moses, she did.

Jesus shed the first drops of His blood for our salvation in His circumcision. In His great love for us, He came on this earth to save us from our sins and show us the way to Heaven and happiness.

When we are told to do something hard today, let us think of how Jesus and Mary obeyed. Then we will do it well for love of Jesus, and it will bring us a great reward in Heaven.

St. Fulgentius

St. Fulgentius was born of a noble family in Carthage. When he was very young, he was appointed an important officer of the Roman province of Carthage. Fulgentius was not satisfied, for his heart was full of spiritual desires. He decided to become a religious, and in the monastery he entered, he found great peace of mind and heart. Fulgentius was ordained a priest and later became a bishop.

He strongly corrected the heretics of his day with his books and letters. For this reason he was persecuted and exiled to distant lands.

After a life of loving service of God, Fulgentius fell very ill. He gave away all he had to the poor, forgave those who had persecuted him, and died a humble servant of Jesus.

Let us always study our lessons well so that we will know more about our faith, and be able to tell others about Jesus.

JANUARY 3

St. Genevieve

St. Genevieve was born in Paris. While still very young, she desired to devote her life to Jesus. After her parents died, Genevieve went to live with

14

St. Genevieve

her grandmother, where she led a life of prayer and performed works of charity. Genevieve was so pleasing to God that He gave her the power to know the future and to perform miracles.

When the people of Paris were going to run away from a terrible army coming to attack them, Genevieve encouraged them to trust in God. She said that if they did penance, they would be saved. The people did what she said, and the fierce army of Huns suddenly turned back. They did not attack the city at all.

St. Genevieve's life was one of heroic charity and obedience to God's holy will. At the age of eighty-nine, she died in an act of strong and pure love of God. Happily she went to meet Jesus, her Spouse, whom she had served faithfully in life.

One of the best ways for us to help our country is to pray for our leaders, that God may guide them for the good of us all.

January 4

St. Titus

St. Titus, a pagan, became a disciple of St. Paul. Titus labored hard, preaching with St. Paul on his missionary travels. Because of his extraordinary virtue, he was very close to the great Apostle. Paul sent Titus on many missions to the churches, to strengthen the faith and to bring peace when there were arguments among the Christians. It seemed that

St. Titus had a special gift for bringing peace to troubled hearts. And this was another reason why he was dear to St. Paul. When he arrived among a group of Christians, the guilty ones felt sorry, asked forgiveness for what they had done, and accepted the punishment they deserved. After he finished his mission, he would go back to tell St. Paul of his success and so bring him great happiness.

St. Paul made Titus Bishop of Crete and wrote a letter to him there. In it, he called him, "my beloved son." St. Titus died at Crete.

Let us try to imitate this great saint by never quarreling with anyone and by trying to be peacemakers.

≈∾

January 5

St. Simeon the Stylite

St. Simeon was born in Asia Minor of a poor family of shepherds. He became a shepherd like his father. One day, when he was still a young boy, he could not take his sheep out because it was snowing. So he went to church and there heard a reading of the Beatitudes—"Blessed are the poor in spirit . . . ; Blessed are they who mourn . . . ; Blessed are the clean of heart. . . ." Not understanding these words of Jesus, he asked a holy old man for an explanation, and then begged the Lord Himself to teach him how to become perfect. God in His goodness taught Simeon that he must first become very humble and then acquire the other virtues. At once Simeon asked to join a monastery.

Later he went to serve God in a lonely mountain spot, but he was so holy that people kept coming way up there to find him.

At last he had a very tall column built, and on the top of that pillar, he lived for forty years. He is called St. Simeon Stylite, from the word "stylos," which means pillar. There was so little space on that pillar that he could never lie down. What a penance that was!

St. Simeon grew very close to God. He prayed constantly and taught the people who gathered beneath his pillar. Yet, no matter how many special favors God gave him, he never grew proud. He always stayed humble and held a very poor opinion of himself. That is why he became such a great Saint.

Today let us deny ourselves something we like to do very much, so that we, too, may offer some penance to Our Lord to make up for our sins.

January 6

The Epiphany of Our Lord

The Epiphany is the Feast of the visit of the Magi to the Infant Jesus. The Magi were three wise Kings from the East, who made a long trip to adore the King of Kings. When they saw a very unusual star in the sky, they knew that our Savior had been born in Palestine, and they set out to find Him. They did not listen to those who tried to discourage them,

The Epiphany of Our Lord

and they did not mind making the long, hard journey. The three Kings trusted God to lead them by His star.

When they found Jesus with His Mother, Mary, they knelt down and adored Him. Worshipping, they offered Him precious gifts of gold, frankincense, and myrrh. Afterwards, the Magi returned home with their hearts full of joy. They had seen and adored the Son of God.

Let us often visit Jesus in church and receive Him in Holy Communion, even if we have to get up early or walk a long way. In return, Jesus will fill our hearts with joy and give us many graces.

❧

JANUARY 7

St. Lucian

St. Lucian was born in Syria. His rich pagan parents brought him up to worship their false gods. When he was twelve, however, he began to see that his religion was wrong, and after being instructed in the Christian faith, Lucian was baptized. He went away to a Christian school, even though he found it hard to leave home. There he studied Sacred Scripture and began to make mortifications, such as eating very little. Daily he grew closer to God. Lucian became a priest and a teacher of Sacred Scripture himself. When a persecution broke out, the Saint was captured and kept in prison for nine years. There he prepared himself to die for Jesus by reading the Holy Bible.

When brought before the emperor to be judged, Lucian took the opportunity to explain our holy religion to everyone. He suffered patiently, and when they asked him, "Where are you from? Who are your parents?" he only answered, "I am a Christian." He was placed on the rack, and he still repeated these words. Then he was put to death and so he earned the martyr's crown he had long desired.

Let us listen well to the sermons our pastor gives. Our faith will teach us what is right and give us the strength to do it—even when we find it hard.

St. Syncletica

St. Syncletica was a rich young girl who lived in Alexandria, Egypt in the fourth century. When her parents died, they left her and her blind sister a great fortune. But Syncletica gave it to the poor. She kept just enough to live on, and she and her sister devoted themselves to prayer and penance. Hearing of St. Syncletica's great holiness many women came to ask her to teach them how to please God. She was so humble that she felt she was too sinful to teach anyone. At last, however, she did not have the heart to refuse them any longer. and she gave them many wise lessons.

What most surprised everyone who visited the Saint was her great happiness. She who had once been so rich was living on bread and water and sleeping on the ground. Besides that, for three years before her death, she suffered from a very painful sickness. Yet, Syncletica was always joyful and grateful to God for letting her share in the sufferings of His passion. To reward her, three days before her death, the Lord gave her a little idea of the great glory and happiness He had prepared for her in Heaven.

It is not true that to be good we have to be sad. The Saints were always happy. God loves those who serve Him cheerfully.

✿

JANUARY 9

Sts. Julian and Basilissa

Sts. Julian and Basilissa, though they were husband and wife, lived as brother and sister. They turned their home into a hospital in order to help the sick and the poor. St. Julian took care of the men, and St. Basilissa cared for the women. St. Basilissa died after suffering great persecutions for the Faith. Julian lived many years and also received the glorious crown of martyrdom.

Basilissa and Julian spent their whole lives helping others and serving God. They planted the seed of faith by living holy lives and watered it and made it grow with their blood shed for Jesus crucified.

We can imitate these Saints by visiting sick or lonely people to cheer them up and to bring them something good to read.

St. William

St. William came from a wealthy French family, but even as a young boy, he did not care to waste time fooling around or being idle. He spent much time praying. When he joined the Cistercian Order, he was such a good monk that the others were inspired just by looking at him. Yet he always considered himself the least among his brethren.

St. William had a great devotion to Jesus in the Blessed Sacrament. He practiced penance, but he was always very happy. When he was made the Abbot of his community, he remained as humble as ever. At the death of the Archbishop of Bourges, William was chosen to take his place. But so humble was he that he cried on receiving this new honor. Yet he accepted it and did even more penance than before, to convert sinners. Although he loved to be alone with God, he traveled all over his diocese to preach, to visit the poor and the sick, to console them and bring them to Christ. When he died he was buried in ashes, as he had asked.

The more we read about the Saints, the more we find that they really became saints by praying, obeying and doing penance.

St. Theodosius

St. Theodosius was born in Asia Minor. Greatly impressed by the examples of the Patriarch Abraham, of whom he read in the Bible, he decided to imitate him. So he left his family and friends and traveled to Jerusalem to visit all the holy places. While there, he decided to submit himself to a holy hermit named Longinus, so as to serve God by obeying him. Longinus was so pleased with Theodosius' virtues that he entrusted him with the care of a church of Our Lady. Theodosius obeyed promptly, but he grew disturbed by the great admiration the people had for him. He then retired to a mountain and fasted and prayed for years.

Many men were attracted by his holiness and he eventually built a monastery near Bethlehem.

Seeing how good and devout he was, the Patriarch of Jerusalem made Theodosius Superior General of all the religious men living in Palestine. St. Theodosius delighted in helping the poor. He and his monks set more than a hundred tables some days to serve hungry beggars. Even when food was very scarce, and the monks themselves did not have enough, he would not turn the poor people away. Even though he was very active, the Saint kept himself close to God by reading spiritual books often. He lived to be a hundred and five years old.

Let us imitate St. Theodosius' humility by never bragging about ourselves and what we have done.

JANUARY 12

St. Aelred

St. Aelred was master of the household of King David of Scotland. He ardently desired to give himself entirely to God, but he dearly loved his many friends. It was very, very hard for him to leave them, yet in order to belong to God alone, at the age of twenty-four, Aelred entered a Cistercian monastery. There he grew fond of a very holy monk named Simon. One day, forgetting the rule of the monastery forbidding the monks to talk, Aelred spoke to Simon. In great surprise and sorrow, Simon gave him a look he never forgot. From then on, Aelred learned not to let his love for anyone come between him and Jesus.

Later Aelred was made an abbot. He wrote many books on spiritual things. In one of them, he said that we only learn to love God by sharing in His sufferings. Everyone loved St. Aelred because he was so kind and good. And in return he loved everyone for love of Jesus.

St. Aelred died at the age of fifty-seven after having served as abbot for twenty-two years.

We should choose our friends among those who love God and are close to Him. These good friends will help us always to do what is right.

St. Veronica of Milan

St. Veronica was born in a small village near Milan. Her parents were very poor but they were hard working and very pious. Because she was so poor, she never had the chance to learn how to read or write. But she learned from her devout parents how to pray. She prayed always and worked hard to help them.

Veronica wanted to become a nun, but she was very worried because she could not read or write. She used to rise at night to try to teach herself. One day Our Lady appeared to her and told her not to worry, because all she had to know were three things. The first was to be pure in intention, which meant to do all her duties only to please God. The second was to mind her own business and to hate grumbling and criticism. The third was to forget her own troubles in thinking of the sufferings of Jesus every day. Our Blessed Mother's holy advice made Veronica very happy and she tried to practice it.

After preparing herself for three years, Veronica was admitted into the convent of St. Martha of Milan. She was assigned the duty of begging for the daily food. Every moment of her life she tried to obey her superior, because she knew that if she obeyed her superior, she obeyed God.

St. Veronica died a saint at the age of fifty-two.

St. Veronica of Milan

Let us, too, follow Our Lady's advice; that is, let us do everything for the love of Jesus, never complain, and remember each day that Jesus suffered and died for us.

St. Hilary of Poitiers

St. Hilary was born in France and raised a pagan. But he was a very intelligent man, and he thought it was foolish to worship many gods as pagans do. He obtained a copy of the Holy Bible and read it eagerly. There he learned about the one true God and about Jesus Christ Our Savior. At last, Hilary became a Christian.

From his baptism to the end of his life, St. Hilary tried to teach people to believe in God. He also tried to encourage them to lead holy lives. He converted his wife and daughter and later was ordained to the priesthood. He became the Bishop of Poitiers, his city. During this time there was a heresy that said Jesus was not God. St. Hilary showed people how wrong it was.

He wrote many books about the Faith and traveled everywhere preaching that Jesus Christ is truly God. For this he earned the title of Doctor of the Church.

Like St. Hilary, let us be proud of our faith and defend it every time we have a chance.

St. Paul—The First Hermit

St. Paul was born of rich parents in Egypt and became an orphan at the age of fifteen. He had been taught to trust God since he was a very young child. When he was twenty years old, he had to flee to a desert because of a bloody persecution of the Christians. In his great love of God, St. Paul trusted in the Lord to provide him with what he needed to live. He dwelt under a tree that supplied him with fruit for food. A nearby spring gave him water.

When he was one hundred and ten, the great St. Anthony of the Desert went to visit him. St. Anthony tells us how he found out about St. Paul. One day he had a temptation to think that no one else but he had spent his life in the desert as a real hermit. That night God revealed to him that there was another hermit much better than he and so Anthony went to visit him. We are told that while they were talking, a raven dropped a loaf of bread. St. Paul told St. Anthony that for the past sixty years he had been receiving a half a loaf a day. "Now you have come," he said, "and God has doubled the portion. The Lord is truly good!" After they had eaten, they spent the night in prayer.

St. Paul died at the age of one hundred and thirteen, and St. Anthony buried him.

When St. Anthony returned to his monks, he told them: "Sinner that I am, I do not deserve the

St. Paul—the First Hermit

name of monk! I have seen another John the Baptist, another St. Paul in the third Heaven!"

St. Paul spent all his long life in prayer and penance to gain glory in Heaven. Let us, too, spend our time well, because time spent in praying and in doing our duties for Jesus will win us a treasure in Heaven.

St. Honoratus

St. Honoratus' father was a pagan Roman consular. When still very young Honoratus refused to worship the idols of the pagans and became a Christian. He also persuaded his brother Venantius to do the same. Honoratus was very fervent and wanted to live alone with God, but his father had plans to make him great and famous. He tried to change his son's mind by giving him beautiful clothes and everything that he thought could delight him. Yet Honoratus was loyal to Jesus. He kept himself pure always. At last, he was able to leave home. He and Venantius left their riches and went off to serve God. But many people heard of them and came to visit them. With the intention of living alone, they asked a holy hermit, St. Caprais, to be their director, and the three of them left Gaul to set out for a desert. They suffered so much on the journey that Venantius died soon afterwards, and Honoratus himself became very sick. He realized that

31

God willed him to return to France, and so, after he was well enough, he went back and founded a monastery there.

When the Archbishop of Arles died, St. Honoratus was made Archbishop. Although he only lived three years more, everyone loved him for his great charity.

Let us give good example to our younger brothers and sisters, so that they will find it easier to be good.

༄

January 17

St. Anthony of Egypt

St. Anthony was born in a small village in Egypt. When he was twenty years old, his parents died and left him a large estate and the care of his young sister. About six months later, he heard these words of Christ read in church: "If thou wilt be perfect, go sell what thou hast, and give to the poor, and thou shalt have treasure in Heaven: and come, follow Me." Anthony was sure that those words were meant for him. So immediately afterwards, he gave away all that he possessed. His sister entered a convent and Anthony begged an aged hermit to teach him the spiritual life. He also visited other hermits to learn and practice each one's most outstanding virtue. Then he began his own life of prayer and penance alone with God.

When he was fifty-five, St. Anthony built a monastery to help others. He was the first to establish the religious life as it is today. Many people heard of him and sought his advice. He would tell them: "The devil is afraid of us when we pray and make sacrifices, when we are humble and good, but especially when we love Jesus very much. He runs away when we make the Sign of the Cross."

St. Anthony visited Paul the hermit and came away holier than ever. He died at the age of one hundred and five.

We must never become discouraged when the devil strongly tempts us to do wrong. Jesus is right beside us. If we pray to Him, He will help us, and He will reward us for our love and faithfulness.

JANUARY 18

Chair of St. Peter at Rome

St. Peter was the Prince of the Apostles and the first Pope. After Jesus went back to Heaven, St. Peter preached the Gospel and ruled the Church, as Jesus had told him to do. At first, he labored in Jerusalem and in Antioch, two big cities of the East. Later, he went to preach the Gospel in Rome. Rome, the great capital of the world, was a wicked pagan city. But there, with the help of God, St. Peter soon brought many souls to Jesus.

F. Nagni

St. Peter

The Feast of St. Peter's Chair at Rome reminds us of the great Church St. Peter founded in that city. St. Peter was martyred for the faith, but down through the ages there has always been a Bishop of Rome. He is the Pope and he rules the whole Church, as St. Peter did, in the name of Jesus. We call the successor of St. Peter the *Holy Father*.

We love and honor the Pope because he takes the place of Jesus on earth. Let us always pray for our Holy Father, that God may give him strength, light and consolation.

❧

JANUARY 19

St. Canute

St. Canute was a strong, wise king of Denmark. He was a great athlete, an expert horseman, and a marvelous general.

At the beginning of his reign, he led a war against the barbarians and defeated them. Everywhere he conquered, he brought the Christian faith. In gratitude for his glorious victories, St. Canute knelt at the foot of the altar and offered his crown to the King of Kings, Jesus.

He was very charitable and gentle to his people. He tried to help them with their problems. Most of all, he wanted to make them true followers of Jesus.

However, a rebellion broke out in his kingdom because of the laws he had made about supporting the Church. One day his enemies went to the church where Canute was praying. He knew they had come to harm him. At the foot of the altar, he made his confession and received Holy Communion. With all his heart he forgave his enemies. Then, as he prayed, a spear was thrown through a window and killed him.

As St. Canute offered his royal crown to Jesus for all he had received, we, too, should thank God every day and offer Him a crown made up of good deeds.

St. Sebastian

St. Sebastian was born in France, but his parents were from Milan, Italy, and he was raised as a Christian in that city.

In order to help his fellow Christians who were dying as martyrs, he went to Rome and enlisted in the army. He became an officer and a great favorite of the Emperor Diocletian. Diocletian made him a captain. In this position, Sebastian converted many to Jesus. When the twin brothers, Mark and Marcellinus were put in prison for the faith, their pagan family kept trying to persuade them to deny Jesus. The two brothers were finding it hard to remain strong. But Sebastian came to encourage them, and they went bravely to their martyrdom. What is more, their family became Christians, too. And Sebastian also converted the jailor and sixty-four

St. Sebastian

prisoners! At last, a false disciple betrayed him to the Emperor. Diocletian tried in every way to make his captain Sebastian give up the Christian faith, but he would not. Then the Emperor accused him of being ungrateful. He called him a traitor. "I am not disloyal to you," answered Sebastian. "I am very faithful to you and grateful. That is why I am praying to the true God for you and for the Roman Empire." But in anger Diocletian ordered Sebastian to be killed with arrows.

The archers shot arrows into every part of the brave soldier's body and then left him for dead. When a holy widow came to bury him, she found him still alive. She took him to her home and nursed his wounds. When Sebastian was well enough, the widow tried to persuade him to escape, but Sebastian was a brave soldier of Christ and he would not leave. Instead he went out to meet the Emperor and urged him to stop his persecution of the Christians.

The Emperor was greatly shocked to see Sebastian alive. At once he ordered him to be beaten with clubs until dead.

So it was that St. Sebastian suffered two martyrdoms.

We should always encourage our friends to do good. This is the best way to be a real friend to others.

JANUARY 21

St. Agnes

St. Agnes was a Roman girl who was only thirteen years old when she suffered martyrdom for her Faith. Agnes had made a promise to God never to stain her purity. Her love for the Lord was very great and she hated sin even more than death! Since she was very beautiful, many young men wished to marry Agnes, but she would always say, "Jesus Christ is my only spouse."

Procop, the Governor's son, became very angry when she refused him. He had tried to win her for his wife with rich gifts and promises, but the beautiful young girl kept saying, "I am already promised to the Lord of the Universe. He is more splendid than the sun and the stars, and He has said He will never leave me!" In great anger, Procop accused her of being a Christian and brought her to his father, the Governor. The Governor promised Agnes wonderful gifts if she would only deny God, but Agnes refused. He tried to change her mind by putting her in chains, but her lovely face shown with joy. Next he sent her to a place of sin, but an Angel protected her. At last, she was condemned to death. Even the pagans cried to see such a young and beautiful girl going to death. Yet, Agnes was as happy as a bride on her wedding day. She did not pay attention to those who begged her to save herself. "I would offend my Spouse," she said, "if I were to try to please you. He chose me first and He shall have

39

St. Agnes

me!" Then she prayed and bowed her head for the death-stroke of the sword.

If we are careful about what we look at, it will be easier to keep our heart pure for love of God.

St. Vincent of Saragossa

St. Vincent was a Spanish deacon. Because he preached about God, he was put into prison and tortured without mercy.

First, he was tied to a red-hot iron and scourged with iron hooks. Then salt was rubbed into his open wounds. But while all this was going on, St. Vincent kept his eyes raised to Heaven in constant prayer. The courageous saint was next cast into prison without food or visitors.

Later the Christians were permitted to come to visit Vincent in jail and they took care of him. They kissed his wounds and took home clothes dipped in his blood as relics.

When St. Vincent died, the emperor ordered his body to be left for animals to destroy, but God protected it. Then the ruler had it tied to a heavy stone and thrown into the sea. But again God worked a miracle to honor St. Vincent. His body floated on top of the water and when the waves brought it ashore, the Christians buried it and built a large church over it.

Let us, too, learn to offer up our little sufferings bravely for the love of Jesus.

St. Raymond of Pennafort

Born in Spain, St. Raymond was a relative of the King of Aragon. From childhood he had a tender love and devotion to the Blessed Mother. Raymond finished his studies at an early age, and became a famous teacher. Then he gave up all his honors and entered the order of the Dominicans. St. Raymond was very humble and very close to God. He did much penance and was so good and kind that he won many sinners to God. With King James of Aragon and St. Peter Nolasco he founded the order of Our Lady of Ransom. The brave religious of this Order devoted themselves to saving poor Christians captured by the Moors.

Once he went with King James to the Island of Majorca to preach about Jesus. King James was a man of great qualities, but he let himself be ruled by passions. There on the Island, too, he was giving bad example. The Saint commanded him to send the woman away. The King said he would, but he did not keep his promise. So St. Raymond decided to leave the island. The King declared he would punish any ship captain who brought the saint back to Barcelona. Putting all his trust in God, St. Ray-

St. Raymond of Pennafort

mond spread his cloak upon the water, tied up one corner of it to a stick for a sail, made the Sign of the Cross, stepped onto the cloak, and sailed along for six hours until he reached Barcelona. This miracle moved the King. He was sorry for what he had done, and he became a true follower of St. Raymond.

When we have done wrong, we must be sorry at once, and make up our minds not to sin again.

JANUARY 24

St. Timothy

St. Timothy was born in Asia Minor. His father was a pagan and his mother a Hebrew. When St. Paul went to preach in his city, the lad Timothy, his mother and his grandmother all became Christians. Several years later, St. Paul came back and found Timothy now a young man, whom people said would do great things. St. Paul saw that he would make a good missionary and the young man was eager to go with him. So it was that Timothy left his home and his parents to follow St. Paul, to share in his sufferings and to bring the word of God to many people. St. Timothy was the great Apostle's beloved disciple. He was his dear son in Christ, faithful always. St. Paul once said that he had no one else like him. He went everywhere with St. Paul, until the Apostle made him Bishop of the great city of Ephesus. It was very hard for St. Timothy to be far away from Paul, but he made the sacrifice for the love of God. Before he was martyred, St. Paul wrote Timothy a beautiful letter from his prison cell in Rome. He encouraged him to become a saint, to read the Bible and to try to please God. He wanted him to pay no attention to busybodies, and to give good example to everyone.

As St. Paul, Timothy, too, died a martyr. He was beaten and stoned to death because he opposed the worship of false gods.

Let us not be busybodies or "chatterboxes". Like St. Timothy, let us read holy books in order to be able to know and love God more.

JANUARY 25

The Conversion of St. Paul

Paul was first called Saul. As a young man, he was a very bright student of the Hebrew religion. When he grew older, he persecuted the followers of Jesus in Jerusalem because he did not know Jesus was God. It was he who held the robes of the men who stoned to death the first martyr, St. Stephen. But one day when he was on his way to hunt down more Christians in the city of Damascus, a great light suddenly shone all around him. As he fell from his horse, he heard a voice say, "Saul, Saul, why do you persecute Me?"

And Saul asked, "Who art thou, Lord?"

The Conversion of St. Paul

Our Lord answered, "I am Jesus, Whom you are persecuting. It is hard for you to kick against the goad."

Afraid and trembling, Saul said, "Lord, what will you have me do?"

At that moment, Saul became a great lover of Jesus. After his baptism, he thought only of making everyone know and love the Lord Jesus, our Savior.

We know Saul by his Roman name of Paul. He is the great Apostle who travelled all over the world, preaching about Jesus and converting millions of people in one city after another.

He worked and suffered, and his enemies tried to take his life many times. Yet nothing could stop him from bringing souls to Christ. When he was old and tired, he was once again put in prison and sentenced to die. Still St. Paul was happy to suffer for Christ.

This great Apostle wrote fourteen marvellous letters to the Christians. They are in the Holy Bible. These letters, called Epistles, are read almost every morning at Holy Mass.

God asks us, too, to love Jesus very much. Do we often tell Our Lord that we love Him?

JANUARY 26

St. Polycarp

St. Polycarp was a beloved disciple of St. John the Evangelist. Like St. John he was good and kind to everyone, but he avoided the company of bad men. Once when someone was preaching something different from what Our Lord said, Polycarp plugged his ears! All that he learned from St. John, he taught to others. When Christians were being put to death, St. Polycarp, too, was captured. He gave a meal to the men who came to capture him and then asked them to let him pray awhile. The judge tried to make him save himself from death by cursing Jesus. "I have served Jesus eighty-six years," answered the Saint, "and He has never done me any wrong. How can I curse my King who died for me?"

The soldiers tied St. Polycarp's hands behind his back and placed him on a burning pile. But the fire did not harm him! One of the soldiers then stabbed a lance into his heart. And so the holy martyr went to be forever with the Divine Master he had served so well.

Let us at once break off a friendship with anyone who gives bad example, and let us keep only good friends. Their example will help us to be the kind of boys and girls Jesus wants.

❦

JANUARY 27

St. John Chrysostom

St. John Chrysostom was born at Antioch. His father died when he was a baby and his good young mother did not want to marry again. She gave all

St. John Chrysostom

her attention to bringing up her son and daughter in the holy love of God. She made many sacrifices so that John could have the best teachers. He was very intelligent and could have become a great man in the world. When he gave speeches everyone loved to listen to him. In fact, his name, Chrysostom, means "Golden-mouthed." Yet, John wanted to give himself to God. He became a priest and later was made Bishop of the great city of Constantinople.

St. John was a wonderful bishop. Although he was always sickly, he accomplished a tremendous amount of good. He preached once or twice every day, fed the poor, took care of orphans, corrected bad customs, and stopped bad plays from being given. He loved everyone, but he was not afraid to tell even the Empress when she did wrong.

Because he fought sin, St. John had enemies— the Empress was one. She had him sent away from Constantinople and on the trip he suffered greatly from fever, from lack of food and sleep. Yet, he was happy to suffer for Jesus and just before he died, he cried out, "Glory be to God!"

A terrible hailstorm fell on Constantinople at his death and four days later, the bad Empress died. Her son honored St. John's body and showed how sorry he was for what his parents had done.

God sees us all the time. If we do everything well and for Him, then we do not have to be afraid of what others say or do against us.

St. Peter Nolasco

St. Peter Nolasco was born in France. Even while he was just a boy, he found great joy in helping the poor. He loved the Blessed Virgin with all his heart and made up his mind to spend his life serving his neighbor. St. Peter felt especially sorry for all the Christians who had been dragged off as slaves by the Moslems. He prayed hard for them, and the Blessed Mother appeared to tell him to start a Religious Order to help them. She said it would please her and Jesus very much, and she would protect the new religious. When St. Peter told his Confessor, St. Raymond of Pennafort, he found that Our Lady had appeared to him, too. Together they went to tell the King, but they were surprised to learn that he, too, had seen the Blessed Mother! So, all three dedicated themselves to the new work of mercy. They promised to do all they could to free the slaves, even if they had to sacrifice their own lives.

Right from the beginning, a great number of slaves were freed, not only in Spain, but also in Africa. St. Peter was not afraid to risk his life many times to come to the rescue of the poor prisoners.

The person who sins becomes a slave of the devil. When temptations come, let us ask our Blessed Mother to help us, so that we may win over the devil and remain faithful to our Divine King.

St. Francis de Sales

While in school, this young Frenchman received the highest honors. His greatest joy was to be with God in prayer, and when he was given time to play, he would read the lives of the Saints and reflect on their love for God.

St. Francis gave up the chance to be a great man in the eyes of the world, for he wanted to be a priest. He wanted to become great in the eyes of God.

At that time there were many people who had lost the true faith. Francis set out to convert them. He went on foot with a Bible, a breviary and one companion, his cousin, Father Louis de Sales. Every place they went, they met people who wanted to kill them. They were insulted and made to suffer. Yet, they did not turn back. And, after four years of hard work, the Saint had converted 72,000 souls! He gave all the credit to God, Who had given him the power to preach and convert.

St. Francis once had a very hot temper, but after praying and trying to correct this fault, he finally became a model of gentle meekness.

He became Bishop of Geneva and founded the Order of the Visitation. He also wrote wonderful books that teach everyone how to grow holy. As Bishop, he lived in a very simple house and practiced mortification. He sacrificed himself to help everyone.

Once, a group of men came to ask his help. They lived in a town high in the mountains. Part of a mountain had fallen and blocked off the road leading to their town. They needed someone to go to see what had happened and then tell the King. "I'll go at once," said the Saint. The men were so surprised! A bishop would come to climb over those rocks just to help them! Yes, St. Francis de Sales would do anything to help people.

After a life spent in good works, this kindly Saint died. Pope Pius IV gave him the title of Doctor of the Church.

To keep peace with everyone, we will watch our words. Those who do not sin with the tongue, says the Apostle St. James, are saints.

January 30

St. Bathildes

Born in England, St. Bathildes was taken to France and sold as a slave while she was still a young girl. She was bought for a very cheap price by the mayor of the Palace. As she grew older, she became very wise and virtuous. She was so gentle and good that King Clovis married her and made her Queen Bathildes. Three sons were born to her, but the King died when the oldest was still just a little boy. So, St. Bathildes ruled the Kingdom until they grew up.

She used her new honor to help the Church in every way she could. She did not become proud or unkind. Rather, this good Queen cared for the poor, forbade that Christians be made slaves, filled France with hospitals for the sick and founded a seminary and a convent.

Later she entered the convent herself. There she forgot her royal dignity and became very obedient and humble. She showed great charity to the sick. When she became ill, she suffered long and patiently until her death.

Because St. Bathildes was never selfish, she became a great saint. By sharing our things, we will make others happy and win much glory in Heaven.

෴

JANUARY 31

St. John Bosco

St. John Bosco was born near Turin, Italy. Like many Saints, he was a poor farm lad, who was brought up by his holy mother in the love of God and Our Lady. John's father died when he was young and his mother had to work very hard to feed her family. John, too, worked as hard as he could to help his mother. He was an intelligent lad, who knew how to keep his playmates from offending God. He would do tricks to win their attention and then he would talk to them about spiritual things.

In order to become a priest, John had to work his way through school. He did all kinds of work.

St. John Bosco

He was a carpenter, a shoemaker, a cook, a pastry-maker, a farmer, and many other things. At the same time he was a fine student and was always happy and cheerful.

After he became a priest, Don Bosco, which means Father Bosco, began his great mission of helping orphan boys. He gathered together hundreds of these boys who had no home. He taught them all kinds of work, so that they would not steal and get into trouble. At first, people were angry with Don Bosco, because they did not think those boys would turn out to be good. But he proved that they would.

"Do you want to be Don Bosco's friend?" he would ask each new boy who came to him. "You do? Then, you must help me save your soul." Every night, he wanted his boys to say three *Hail Marys*, so that the Blessed Mother would help them avoid sin. He also recommended that they go to Confession and Communion as often as possible.

One of Don Bosco's boys became a saint, St. Dominic Savio.

Later on, Don Bosco founded two Religious Orders to take care of poor children and he also built many homes and schools for them.

Let us help our parents at home as much as we can. The more things we learn to do, the better we can serve God.

꿍

FEBRUARY 1

St. Bridget of Ireland

A few years after St. Patrick arrived in Ireland, there was born a little girl called Bridget. Her father was an Irish lord named Duptace.

As Bridget grew up, she became holier and more pious each day. She loved the poor and would often bring food and clothing to them. One day she gave away a whole pail of milk, and then began to worry about what her mother would say. She prayed to the Lord to make up for what she had given away. When she got home, her pail was full!

Bridget was a very pretty young girl, and her father thought that it was time for her to marry. She, however, had given herself entirely to God when she was very small, and she would not think of marrying anyone. When she learned that her beauty was the reason for the attentions of so many young men, she prayed fervently to God to take it from her. She wanted to belong to Him alone. God granted her prayer. Seeing that his daughter was no longer pretty, her father gladly agreed when Bridget asked to become a Sister.

She became the first Religious in Ireland and founded a convent so that other young girls might become Sisters. When she consecrated herself to God, a miracle happened. She became very beauti-

ful again! Bridget made people think of the Blessed
Mother because she was so pure and sweet, so
lovely and gentle. They called her the "Mary of the
Irish."

*Let us not be vain or proud of our appearance.
God looks at our heart, not at our face or our clothes!*

Purification of the Blessed Virgin

Forty days after Jesus was born, Mary and
Joseph brought Him to the Temple to be presented
to the Lord; that was the Law of God and they
obeyed it perfectly.

While they were in the Temple, Mary also ful-
filled another ceremony of the Hebrew Law. After
the birth of their children, all mothers were sup-
posed to go to the Temple for the ceremony called
the Purification. Our Blessed Mother really did not
have to fulfill this ceremony, because she was all
pure. She went anyway, to teach us to be humble
and obedient.

A holy old priest of the Temple named Simeon
learned from God that the Infant Jesus was the
Savior. With what joy he held Mary's Son in his
arms! Then inspired by God, he told her that she
would have to suffer much. He was talking about
the terrible pain our Blessed Mother would feel
when Jesus died on the Cross.

58

Purification of the Blessed Virgin

The Feast of the Presentation and the Purification remind us that we belong to God, first of all. Because He is our Father and Creator, we owe Him our loving obedience.

In imitation of the Blessed Mother, let us cheerfully obey the rules laid down by our parents and teachers.

᪥

FEBRUARY 3

St. Blaise

St. Blaise, as a young man, was a doctor, and a very good one. All the sufferings and troubles he saw made him realize that only spiritual joys can make us really happy. He became a priest and then a Bishop. With all his heart, St. Blaise worked to make his people holy and happy. He prayed and preached; he tried to help everyone.

When the Emperor Licinius began to persecute the Christians, St. Blaise was captured and sent to prison to be beheaded. On the way, people crowded the road to see their beloved bishop for the last time. He blessed them all, even the pagans. A poor mother rushed up and begged him to save her child who was choking to death from a fishbone. The Saint prayed and then worked the miracle. This is why St. Blaise is called upon by all those who have throat diseases. On his feast day, we have our throats blessed, and we ask him to protect us from all sicknesses of the throat.

In prison, the saintly bishop converted many pagans. No torture could make him give up his faith in Jesus. Finally he was beheaded and went to be with Jesus forever.

Today let us honor St. Blaise by going without that candy bar or ice cream cone we planned to have.

FEBRUARY 4

St. Jane Valois

St. Jane was the daughter of King Louis XI of France. Since the King wanted a son, he was very disappointed when Jane was born. Later, he did not even want her to live at the Palace, because she was very short and deformed. When she was five years old, she was sent away to live with other people.

Jane did not want to marry when she grew up because she had given herself to Jesus and His Most Blessed Mother. Her father, however, forced her to marry the Duke of Orleans. Jane was a devoted wife for twenty-two years, but after the Duke became King, he sent Jane to live by herself in a far-off township. The Queen did not complain at such unkindness. She exclaimed, instead: "God be praised! He has permitted this that I may serve Him better than I have up until now."

St. Jane performed many penances and prayed very fervently. She gave all of her money to the poor and founded an Order of Sisters called the Sisters of the Annunciation of the Blessed Virgin Mary.

Let us remember that no matter what a person looks like, what really counts is the goodness in his heart.

~☙~

St. Agatha

Agatha was a beautiful and holy Christian girl of Sicily. When the governor heard of Agatha's beauty, he had her brought to his palace. He wanted to make her commit sins against purity, but she was brave and would not give in. "My Lord Jesus Christ," she prayed, "You see my heart and You know my desire. You alone must have me, because I am all yours. Save me from that evil man. Make me worthy of winning out over the devil."

The governor tried sending Agatha to the house of a wicked woman in the hope that she would change for the worse. But Agatha had great trust in God and prayed all the time. She kept herself pure and would not listen to the evil suggestions of that woman and her daughters. After one month, she was brought back to the governor. He tried again to win her. "You are a noblewoman," he said kindly. "Why have you lowered yourself to be a humble Christian?"

"Even though I am a noble," answered Agatha, "I am a slave of Jesus Christ."

St. Agatha

St. Dorothy

"Then what does it really mean to be noble?" the governor asked.

Agatha answered wisely, "It means to serve God."

When he saw that she would not sin, the governor had her whipped and tortured very cruelly. As she was being carried back to prison she said, "Lord, my Creator, You have protected me from the cradle. You have taken me from the love of the world and given me patience to suffer. Now receive my soul." And with that, her beautiful soul went home to Heaven.

Let us learn from this saint to pray with all our heart when we feel tempted to do wrong.

FEBRUARY 6

St. Dorothy

St. Dorothy was a young and beautiful girl who lived in the city of Caesarea. Both her father and mother died for the Faith. They left her a great deal of money, and Dorothy used it to help poor people and prisoners. Everyone knew her and loved her for her modesty and piety. She was so beautiful and holy that many young men wanted to marry her. But she had given herself to God alone. So they called her, "The Bride of Christ."

When Dorothy herself was put in prison for the Faith, the wicked governor sent two young girls named Crista and Callista to persuade her to deny Jesus. These girls had been Christians once. They had given up their Faith when the governor made them many promises and gave them gifts. But these girls could not change Dorothy. It was she who made them cry for their sin and encouraged them to die bravely for Jesus.

Furious, the governor tortured Dorothy, but she would not worship the gods of Rome. "I cannot worship them or the Emperors either," she said. "I worship only the true God, the Creator of Heaven and earth." At last, the governor gave up The saint was getting the best of him, with her wise answers. So he condemned her to death by beheading.

When Dorothy was on her way to be beheaded, a young pagan made fun of her Faith. "Send me some roses and apples from the garden where you are going after you die," he shouted. Then he laughed cruelly. But St. Dorothy promised that she would. As soon as she died, a child appeared to that pagan carrying three roses and three apples! Where could they have come from? It was not the season for apples and roses! The amazed man realized that the child was an angel come from God and that the flowers and fruit were sent from Heaven. He was converted right then. Soon afterwards, he, too, gave his life for God.

Today let us pray especially for someone who is far away from God, so that he will return to our Heavenly Father.

FEBRUARY 7

St. Romuald

St. Romuald was an Italian nobleman. As a boy, he had many temptations to impurity. In order to avoid falling into sin, he kept himself busy by going hunting in the woods. When Romuald was twenty years old, he was horrified to see his father kill a man in a duel. He went to a Benedictine monastery to do penance for forty days, in reparation for his father's grave sin. Up until that time, he had lived a lazy life of pleasure, but now at the monastery, Romuald was so moved by the good example of the monks that he decided to become one himself. He asked a good monk named Marino to teach him how to become holy. To test him, Marino treated him harshly. Yet Romuald never complained. Later, he founded the Camaldolese Order and gave all his monks a wonderful example of penance. For a whole year, all he ate each day was a bit of boiled beans. Then for three years, he ate only the little food he grew himself. Through these sacrifices Romuald grew closer and closer to God. A hundred times a day, he would pray in his room: "Oh, my sweet Jesus! God of my heart! Delight of pure souls! The object of all my desires!"

When he was over a hundred, St. Romuald had to suffer very much because he was accused of a very bad sin which he had not committed. He did not become angry or take revenge, even when he was not allowed to say Mass for six months. He could easily have proven that it was all a lie. Yet he chose to suffer for love of God until, at last, Jesus Himself showed everyone that Romuald was innocent.

No matter what happens to us, it will turn out for the best, if we love God and pray to Him.

St. John of Matha

St. John of Matha was born in France. He was a happy, pure boy, who loved God and His Blessed Mother very much. His father sent him to school, and John did well in all his studies. As he grew older, many people began coming to him for advice and counsel, and he decided to become a priest so that he could help them more.

When St. John said his first Mass, God showed him that he was to spend his life working to free Christians held as slaves by the Moslems. He founded an Order of priests called Trinitarians to help him in this mission.

St. John's work was blessed by God, and many Christians were freed. Their Moslem owners were very angry with John. But he was not afraid. In fact, he would have liked nothing better than to die a martyr.

Once, when he was going from Africa to Rome, the Moslems tried to sink the ship on which he was traveling. Holding a Crucifix in his hands, John knelt on the deck and began to pray. Soon the ship reached Rome, unharmed!

St. John died two years later.

By often thinking of the great charity of St. John and his priests, we will find it much easier to do good deeds to our neighbor.

❧

St. Apollonia and the Martyrs of Alexandria

In Alexandria, Egypt, during the reign of the Emperor Decius, there lived a holy virgin named Apollonia.

Apollonia had spent her whole life serving God. Now that she was growing old, she did not take time to rest. She bravely risked her life to comfort the Christians in prison when a persecution began.

"Remember that the suffering will not last long," she would say. "But the joys of Heaven will last forever."

At last, Apollonia, too, was captured. When the judge asked her name, she courageously said, "I am a Christian and I love and serve the true God."

Apollonia was made to suffer greatly because she would not give up her Faith. First, all her teeth were smashed and then pulled out. That is why we pray to St. Apollonia when we have a toothache. The Saint was then told that if she did not deny Christ, she would be thrown into the fire.

St. Scholastica

Apollonia was not afraid. She chose to die rather than sin.

When the pagans saw her heroic action, many of them were converted.

The martyrs greatly desired to shed their blood for Christ. And what do we do for Him? Are we strong enough to stand a little suffering for His love?

FEBRUARY 10

St. Scholastica

Scholastica was the twin sister of St. Benedict. For many years, her parents had begged God to send them children. When at last Benedict and Scholastica were born, their good mother did all she could to make them Saints.

Scholastica was a friendly, intelligent girl who promised herself to Jesus when she was still very young. After her parents died, she went to visit her holy brother. He had built a big monastery and was the leader of many good monks.

St. Benedict was very good to his holy sister. When he found out that she and other young women wanted to become religious, he helped her start her convent.

Once a year, St. Benedict came to visit her for one day. On one of his visits, when he was ready to leave the convent, Scholastica begged him to stay longer. Benedict said he could not, but Scholastica knew that soon she would die. So she bowed her head and prayed with all her heart. No sooner had she lifted her head than such a storm arose that Benedict was unable to leave. He stayed and they talked all through the night about the goodness of God and the happiness of the Saints in Heaven. Three days later, when St. Benedict was praying in his monastery, he saw the beautiful soul of his sister Scholastica going up to Heaven in the form of a dove.

Like this saintly brother and sister, let us love one another at home and be of good example to each other.

⤴

FEBRUARY 11

Our Lady of Lourdes

It was on February 11, 1858, that the Blessed Mother first appeared to Bernadette Soubirous, a young girl of Lourdes, France. Bernadette was a sickly, little girl, whose family was so poor they lived in a cellar that had once been a jail. Even though she was fourteen years old, Bernadette could not read or write. She never could remember her catechism lessons, but she was a good girl who loved God very much. And even if her memory was bad, she kept trying hard to learn all she could about God. She was pure and obedient, too. It was to this young girl that our Blessed Mother appeared. The beautiful Lady Bernadette saw wore a white dress with a light blue sash. A white veil covered her head and fell over her shoulders to the ground. On her feet were two lovely golden roses. Her hands were joined and a Rosary hung from her right arm. Its chain and cross shone like gold. The lovely Lady encouraged Bernadette to say the Rosary.

The Blessed Mother appeared eighteen times to St. Bernadette and told her to tell the people to pray, to do penance and often to recite the Rosary for sinners. During the last apparition, Bernadette asked the beautiful Lady who she was. The Lady replied, "I am the Immaculate Conception."

At Lourdes, miracles take place. Many people are cured of sicknesses. Crippled people walk again. Blind people see again. There, where she once appeared to St. Bernadette, Our Lady still shows her love for us.

Let us try to say the Rosary to our Blessed Mother every day. Through this prayer, we receive all the graces we need for ourselves and for those we love.

Seven Holy Founders of the Servite Order

These seven Saints were all young men who lived in Florence, Italy. They had joined a Confraternity in honor of the Blessed Virgin because of their great devotion to her.

On the feast of the Assumption, while they were all deep in prayer, the Blessed Mother appeared to them and inspired them to leave the world and to live alone with God.

After several years of living by themselves, they went to the Bishop to ask for a rule of life. The Bishop told them that the matter was one which needed much prayer. The monks then went back to pray and ask Our Lady to let them know what to do. Mary appeared to them carrying a black habit. At her side was an angel bearing a scroll with the words "Servants of Mary" written on it. In this vision, the Blessed Mother said that she had chosen them to be her servants and to wear the black habit.

These seven wonderful men helped each other to love and serve God better. Together they became great Saints.

Many young men came to join these holy Founders. They were known as Servants of Mary, or Servites.

Like these seven Saints, let us love our Blessed Mother and ask her to help us in every need.

❧

St. Catherine of Ricci

Catherine was born of a very famous family in Florence, Italy. At the age of thirteen, she entered the convent.

Even at that early age, Catherine had a deep love for the Passion of Jesus Christ. She used to

St. Catherine of Ricci

think about Our Lord's sufferings often, and Jesus gave her the great privilege of receiving in her own body the marks of His wounds. She was happy to accept all the sufferings of these wounds.

Catherine also felt very sorry for the Poor Souls in Purgatory. She prayed and did penance for them. Once God let her know that a certain man was in Purgatory. So great was her love that she offered to suffer for him. God listened to her prayer and she suffered greatly for forty days.

At the age of sixty-seven, after a very long and painful illness, St. Catherine joined Jesus, her Beloved Spouse in heaven.

Let us help the poor souls in Purgatory with our prayers, so that they may soon go to Heaven. When they are in Heaven, they will pray for us.

FEBRUARY 14

St. Valentine

Valentine was a holy priest who lived in Rome. Along with St. Marius, he helped the martyrs to die a good and holy death. He gave them the Sacraments of Holy Communion and Extreme Unction to help them on their journey to Heaven.

While he was performing these holy deeds of charity, the Roman soldiers discovered him. But because St. Valentine was admired by all the people— and even by the Emperor—for his virtue and wisdom, he was not put to death at once. The Emperor

St. Valentine

himself sent for him and welcomed him kindly. He invited him to sit down beside him. Then he asked him, "Why did such a wise man as you lower yourself to join a religion that is against the gods of Rome?"

"Sir," answered Valentine gently, "if you knew the God I adore, you would hate the religion that makes you worship devils. You would be proud to adore the only true God, the Creator of Heaven and earth. Only He can make you and all your people truly happy."

The Emperor wanted to know more about the Christian religion, and St. Valentine answered all his questions with great wisdom. The people of the court became angry. They did not like to see their Emperor interested in the religion of the Christians. The Emperor saw that they were angry. He thought more about pleasing men than pleasing God. So he turned the Saint over to the governor to be judged. That is how St. Valentine, too, suffered martyrdom for his beloved Lord Jesus. He was beaten with clubs and later beheaded.

St. Valentine was a man of great virtue because he knew his religion well. The more we learn about our Faith, the more we will want to grow in every virtue.

Sts. Faustinus and Jovita

Sts. Faustinus and Jovita were brothers who lived in Brescia, Italy. From the time they were young, they were famous for their great love for their religion and their works of Christian charity. Never were there two brothers so closely united in zeal for doing good. The bishop of their city made them both priests, and they began to preach everywhere to both the rich and the poor. They spared themselves no sacrifice to bring many to God. They were not afraid of the soldiers, who were putting many Christians to death.

When the Emperor heard that Faustinus and Jovita were preaching openly, he sent them to prison and had them tortured greatly. Yet, no matter what the soldiers made them suffer, Faustinus and Jovita prayed and willingly suffered for the Lord. They would not give up their Faith.

How pleased God is to see brothers and sisters helping one another study their Catechism! May He be pleased with this sight in our home.

February 16

St. Onesimus

St. Onesimus was a slave who robbed his master and ran away to Rome. In Rome he went to see the great Apostle St. Paul, who was a prisoner for his Faith. Paul received Onesimus with fatherly love, made him realize he had done wrong, and converted him to the Faith.

After Onesimus' conversion, St. Paul sent him back to his master, Philemon, who was the Apostle's friend. He sent Philemon a letter, in which he wrote: "I plead with you for my own son, for Onesimus. . . . I am sending him back to you. Welcome him as though he were my very heart."

Onesimus returned home and was set free. Later, he went back to St. Paul and became his faithful helper.

St. Paul made Onesimus a priest and then Bishop of Ephesus. During the persecutions, he was brought in chains to Rome and there stoned to death.

If we ever should hurt anyone in any way, let us ask forgiveness right away. God will be pleased to see that we are sorry and He will bless us as He did Onesimus.

St. Gerard Majella

As a young boy, Gerard showed his love for Jesus by doing all he could to help the poor. He went to work so that he would have money to buy them food and clothes. Once he gave a beggar a brand new suit he himself really needed.

Gerard dearly loved Jesus in the Blessed Sacrament and the Blessed Virgin Mary. He wanted to become a religious to serve them all his life. But he had a very hard time trying to enter religious life, because he was sickly. Besides that, his mother and his sisters absolutely did not want him to go. Still he kept trying. At last he was accepted as a brother in the Redemptorist Order.

"Let me do it! I am the youngest," Brother Gerard would say whenever there was hard, lowly work to be done. Everyone loved and admired this good, humble brother.

"I want only what God wants for me," St. Gerard often exclaimed. And he was happy when he had something to suffer for Jesus.

Whoever is called to become a priest, a brother, or a sister should trust in God and follow his vocation, no matter how hard a time he has.

St. Bernadette

St. Bernadette

St. Bernadette was born at Lourdes, France. Her parents were very poor and she herself was in poor health.

One Thursday, February 11, 1858, when she was sent with her younger sister and a friend to gather firewood, a very beautiful Lady appeared to her above a rosebush in a grotto called Massabielle. The lovely Lady was dressed in blue and white. She smiled at Bernadette and then made the sign of the cross with a rosary of ivory and gold. Bernadette fell on her knees, took out her own rosary and began to say it.

The beautiful Lady was God's Mother, the Blessed Virgin Mary. She appeared to Bernadette seventeen other times and spoke with her. She told Bernadette that she should pray for sinners, do penance and have a chapel built there in her honor.

Many people did not believe Bernadette when she spoke of her vision. She had to suffer much. But one day Our Lady told Bernadette to dig in the mud. As she did, a spring of water began to flow. The next day it continued to grow larger and larger. Many miracles happened when people began to use this water.

When Bernadette was older, she became a sister. She was always very humble. More than anything else, she desired not to be praised. Once a sister asked her if she had temptations of pride because she was favored by the Blessed Mother. "How can I?" she answered quickly. "The Blessed Virgin chose me only because I was the most ignorant." What humility!

Today let us pray to Our Lady and make some little sacrifice for the conversion of sinners.

⤣

FEBRUARY 19

St. Barbatus

St. Barbatus was born in Italy. He was given a Christian education and was a very good and devout boy. What he liked most to do was to read the Holy Bible. As soon as he was old enough he was ordained a priest and later made pastor. But some of the people did not like him to tell them that they must lead better lives and be sorry for their sins. So they persecuted him and obliged him to leave.

St. Barbatus went back to Benevento, where he was born. There he was received with great joy. Many people in this city were converts to Christianity, but they still kept pagan idols in their homes. And they still believed that these idols had magic powers. St. Barbatus preached against this custom, but the people did not want to give up the false gods. The Saint told them that because of this sin, their city would be attacked by their enemies, and it was.

Afterwards, the people gave up their error and peace returned. St. Barbatus was made Bishop and continued his work to convert his people.

Our parish priests, like St. Barbatus, want us to be good so that we will go to Heaven. Let us listen to their advice and follow it.

St. Eucherius

St. Eucherius was born at Orleans, France. Every day his mother would offer him to God, and he was given a very good education. A sentence from the letters of St. Paul made a big change in him. The sentence was: "This world, as we see it, is passing away." It made him realize that our lives on this earth are very short and that Heaven and Hell last forever. He decided then and there to earn the joys of Heaven by living for God alone.

So Eucherius left his rich home and entered the Benedictine Abbey. There he spent seven years in close union with God.

After the death of his uncle, the Bishop of Orleans, he was chosen to take his place as Bishop. Eucherius was then only twenty-five and he was very humble. He did not want to leave his beloved Abbey. With tears, he begged to be allowed to remain alone with God in the monastery. But finally, he gave in for love of obedience. Eucherius became a holy, wise Bishop and did much good to his priests and to his people.

Charles Martel, who was Mayor of the Palace, used to take some of the Church's money to use for war. Because Bishop Eucherius told him that was wrong, Charles had him taken prisoner.

But the governor in whose charge he put him was so moved by Eucherius' meekness toward his enemies that some time later, he sent him back to a monastery.

Here, the Saint spent all his time in prayer until his death.

Let us, too, remember what St. Paul says: "This world is passing away," and try to think more of Heaven.

❧

St. Dositheus

This Saint was the son of a Roman general, who gave him whatever he wanted. Dositheus was tall and handsome, and he lived a life of fun in his rich house. He knew nothing about his religion. One day he decided to go with some officers on a trip to Jerusalem. There he saw where Jesus had walked and preached and suffered. In one church he also saw a picture representing Hell.

"What is that?" he asked. When he found out, what torments the damned souls suffer there, he could not get it out of his mind. He began to pray and to live a holy life. His friends could not believe their eyes! "You are living like a monk in a monastery!" one said. Dositheus wondered what a monastery was. At last, to please him, they took him to the monastery where St. Seridon was the abbot. Dositheus asked to be allowed to enter, because he said he wanted to save his soul.

As a monk, Dositheus obeyed perfectly. He did whatever he was told and grew holier every day. Once, to test him, his director had him make a habit for himself and then told him to give it to another. Three or four times he did that. Yet St. Dositheus did not complain once.

Only five years did this young man live as a monk. When he was just twenty-two, he caught a very bad sickness, which soon took his life. He had not been able to do great penances either, because of his poor health. Yet, he became a Saint in that short time by obeying perfectly.

Let us try to imitate St. Dositheus by obeying quickly and cheerfully always. Whoever obeys is sure of doing what God wants.

St. Margaret of Cortona

Little Margaret was only eight when her mother died. Her father married another woman, who treated her harshly.

At the age of sixteen, Margaret met a rich young man, who was struck by her beauty. He told her that

St. Margaret of Cortona

he loved her. The poor girl was unhappy at home and she wanted to be loved. She wanted a grand house instead of a poor cottage. She thought it would be so nice to wear beautiful gowns and jewels instead of ragged clothes. So she went off with the noble-man.

Although she now had the things she wanted, Margaret was never really happy. Deep down in her heart she felt bad because she was leading a life of sin.

One day, the nobleman was killed in the woods. His dog came home and led Margaret to the place where he lay. As she looked down on his body, she realized that if she did not change her sinful life she might one day die without God's grace. That terrible sight made such an impression on her that then and there, at only twenty-five years of age, she made up her mind to change. She confessed her sins and did penance for the rest of her life. To make up for the bad example she had given, she once put a rope around her neck and begged forgiveness to everyone in her parish church.

Her father and stepmother would not let her live in her home, but Margaret put all her trust in her heavenly Father. She started a hospital for the sick poor and served there herself. She brought many souls to God by her good example.

If we have given bad example, we should ask God's pardon. Then let us make up for our faults by kind words and good deeds.

St. Serenus

St. Serenus was a Greek who left all his belongings and went to Yugoslavia to live a holy life. He lived alone and grew just enough fruit and vegetables to live on.

One night he awoke to hear someone in his garden. Getting up to find out who it was, he saw a woman and asked her what she was doing. She answered that she liked to walk in his garden.

But St. Serenus knew that she was a bad woman and he told her to leave. The lady was very angry when she left. She went to her husband, who was one of the Emperor Maximian's guards. She told him that Serenus had insulted her.

Her husband believed the lie and wrote to the governor of the land to punish Serenus.

When the governor called Serenus, he found out that it was really the woman who was evil, not Serenus. Just as the Saint was about to be freed, someone said to the governor that such a holy man might be a Christian. At that time, the Christians were being persecuted. The governor asked Serenus if he were a Christian. Serenus was happy to declare his faith in Jesus and to have the privilege of dying a martyr.

If we have any friends who are not good, we will not go with them any more. It is better to be alone than to be with bad companions.

FEBRUARY 24

St. Matthias the Apostle

St. Matthias was one of Our Lord's seventy-two disciples. He was good and pure as a boy and as a young man. So when he met Jesus, he was attracted to Him and followed Him.

He was with Our Lord during His whole public life.

After Jesus had gone back to Heaven, the eleven Apostles met together to choose another to take the place of Judas the traitor. They prayed to God to show them whom He had chosen. Then they cast lots and Matthias was the one chosen. He received the Holy Spirit with the other Apostles.

St. Matthias was a very good Apostle and preached the Word of God to many people. At last the enemies of Jesus grew so furious to see how people listened to Matthias that they put him to death. The Martyr thanked Jesus for letting him die for Him, and then he prayed for his enemies.

Matthias had lived a very holy life and Jesus welcomed his faithful Apostle into the joys of Heaven.

Every morning, let us ask Jesus to give us the grace of living and dying faithful to Him.

St. Walburga

St. Walburga came from a family of Saints. Her father was St. Richard. Her brothers were St. Willibald and St. Winebald. She herself entered the convent after she had finished her education.

St. Walburga's brother went with St. Boniface to convert Germany.

Later her brother founded a monastery with two houses, one for monks and the other for sisters. St. Walburga was asked to take care of the sisters while her brother took care of the monks. After his death, St. Walburga took care of both.

The pagans greatly admired these holy women who worked so hard on their convent farms. They listened to what the monks and nuns taught them about Christ, because they saw what holy lives they were living. Besides all her other duties, St. Walburga also took care of the pagans when they fell sick.

When she, too, went to Heaven, she was buried beside her brother.

Let us offer prayers and sacrifices so that everyone in our family may live as good Christians and save their souls.

St. Porphyry

Born of wealthy and noble parents, Porphyry left his family when he was twenty-five. He went to Egypt to enter a monastery. After five years, he made a trip to Jerusalem to visit the places where Jesus had been when He was on earth.

Porphyry loved the poor. He sold everything he had in order to help those in need.

At the age of forty he became a priest and was given care of the relics of the true Cross of Jesus.

When Porphyry was made bishop of Gaza, he worked as hard as he could to convert the pagans and stop the many pagan practices and superstitions.

Although he was able to stop many of these practices, he had to suffer very much from his enemies.

Let us have nothing to do with foolish superstitions. There is no such thing as good luck from charms or bad luck from numbers, and other such things. God watches over us and gives us all the help we need, if we pray.

St. Gabriel of Our Lady of Sorrows

This lovable Saint was born at Assisi and received the name Francis at Baptism, in honor of the

St. Gabriel of Our Lady of Sorrows

great St. Francis of Assisi. His mother died when he was only four. Francis' father sent for a governess to raise him and the other children.

Francis grew to be a very handsome, likeable boy, who was the most popular dancer at all the parties. He really loved to have fun, but he was a good boy and even while having good times, he felt bored. He felt in his heart a strong desire for the things of God. Twice when he became so sick that he nearly died, he promised Our Lady that if she obtained his cure, he would become a religious. He did get better both times, but he did not keep his promise.

One day, afterwards, as he looked at a picture of the Sorrowful Mother being carried in a procession, it seemed to him that the Blessed Mother looked at him. At the same time, he felt something like a voice in his heart telling him: "Francis, the world is not for you any more."

That did it. Francis entered the Passionist monastery. He was only eighteen. The name he took was Gabriel of the Sorrowful Mother.

Gabriel's three great loves were the Passion of Our Lord, the Blessed Sacrament and our Sorrowful Mother.

He practiced two virtues in a special way: humility and obedience. In just six years, Gabriel became a saint.

We should not think only of having good times. God made us for Heaven. So we should often think of the great joys awaiting us there, if we live a life pleasing to God.

Sts. Romanus and Lupicinus

St. Romanus was a French youth who was admired by everyone for his goodness. He had a great desire to become a saint. Since he saw that in the world there are many dangers for our soul's salvation, he decided to go to live alone with God. First, he asked advice of a holy monk, and then he started off. He took with him two books on the lives of the saints. Living by himself, he thought continually about God, and praised and thanked Him.

Soon afterwards, his brother Lupicinus joined him. Romanus and Lupicinus were very different in their ways. Romanus was very hard on himself but very kind and gentle and full of understanding with others. Lupicinus was hard and severe with himself and with everybody else, too. Yet they got along perfectly.

When many men came to join them, they built two monasteries. Romanus governed one and Lupicinus governed the other.

They prayed much and did much penance. They worked very hard, kept silent all the time, and were concerned only about becoming Saints.

St. Romanus and St. Lupicinus were both Saints, even though they were so different. We should learn never to dislike anyone, for everyone has many good qualities.

❧

MARCH 1

St. Eudocia

Eudocia was a very beautiful young woman who loved rich clothes and jewels. People called her the most beautiful woman of her times. She lived a carefree, sinful life in her rich house in Egypt. One night she awoke because the sound of singing was coming from the next house. After the singing stopped, she heard the same voice reading aloud about what sinners suffer in hell, and what the Saints enjoy in Heaven. Eudocia was so frightened that she could not sleep any more. The next morning she found out that the strange voice was a monk's. He was the guest of her neighbor and had gotten up at night, as he always did, to praise God and pray. She asked him to come to explain to her what he had read. When she began to cry over her sins, the holy monk told her not to be discouraged. He told her to start leading a good life from then on.

Eudocia was taught all about the Christian religion and was then baptized. Right afterwards she freed all her slaves. She encouraged them to become Christians, too. No more did she care for money and beautiful clothes. She gave away all she had and left her rich house. From then on, she became a model Christian because of the great virtue she practiced.

Eudocia went off to live alone and serve Jesus with prayer and penance. She ended her life by gaining the crown of martyrdom during the Emperor Trajan's persecution of Christians.

When we make the resolution to become better, the devil trys to make us break it. Let us never listen to him. Instead, we must pray and go to Confession and Communion often. Then we will be strong enough to overcome every temptation.

MARCH 2

St. Simplicius

St. Simplicius was a Pope. In his day, great numbers of the people had many wrong ideas about the Christian faith. And many, many others were pagans. St. Simplicius was alone in trying to correct these evils. But since he was both learned and holy, he never gave up. More than by words, he taught with the example of his holy life. And always he corrected others with charity and humility. Yet his good, fatherly heart had to suffer very much because some Christians stubbornly held on to their wrong opinions. Then with great sorrow, St. Simplicius had to put them out of the Church.

He was Pope for fifteen years and eleven months. Then Our Lord called him to receive the reward of his labors.

Let us be grateful to those who correct us, even when it hurts, because they are the ones who love us.

❧

MARCH 3

St. Cunegundes

St. Cunegundes was the daughter of a King. She was married to the Emperor, St. Henry II. This holy couple led virgin lives, like brother and sister. Even though she was the Empress, St. Cunegundes spent a great deal of her time in prayer and in works of charity. She gave up all the good times she could have had in the palace. She visited the poor and the sick in the hospitals and also cared for lepers.

St. Cunegundes and her husband, St. Henry loved each other very much. They never quarrelled. And they gave one another good example in the practice of every virtue. But the devil was jealous of their goodness and he tried to cause trouble between them. Wicked people accused the Empress of having committed a shameful sin. Since she remained silent about it, her husband believed them and felt very bad. For this reason, she asked to be permitted to go through the trial by fire, according to the custom of those days. She walked barefoot on red-hot pieces of metal for quite some time. Yet she was not burned at all! By this miracle God showed her husband and all the people that she was innocent.

St. Cunegundes

When her husband, St. Henry, died, Cunegundes sold all that she owned and gave it to the poor. Then she followed the call of Christ to the convent.

There, for fifteen years, she was the most humble and obedient of all the nuns. She seemed to have forgotten completely that she was ever an Empress. She even begged her Superiors to give her the hardest and most lowly work to do.

St. Cunegundes was made Patroness of Poland.

We can always keep ourselves pure, even in the midst of many dangers. But we have to pray and to avoid bad companions, bad books and magazines, bad movies and TV shows. We also have to mortify our senses, especially our eyes and our sense of touch—whether we are alone or with others.

MARCH 4

St. Casimir of Poland

St. Casimir was one of the thirteen children of the King of Poland. With the help of his virtuous mother and his devout tutor, Casimir grew in wisdom and virtue.

At the age of thirteen he had the chance to become king, but he refused. The rest of his life he spent in trying to become a saint. He was always cheerful and friendly with everyone. He fasted, slept on the ground and prayed in the middle of the night. He loved to meditate on the Passion of Jesus, which is a good way of learning to love our God,

Who loves us so much. Casimir also loved the Blessed Virgin with a special love. In her honor he loved to recite a beautiful hymn very often. We have a part of it in English and it is called, "Daily, Daily, Sing to Mary."

Casimir was never too healthy, yet he was courageous and strong in character. He would always do what he knew was right. Sometimes he would even advise his father, the King, to rule the people fairly. He always did this with great respect, and his father would listen to him.

St. Casimir had a great love for virginity. Even though his parents found a very beautiful and virtuous young woman for him to marry, he chose to give his heart to God alone.

St. Casimir died when he was still very young.

Even if we are not too strong or healthy, we can still be strong in character. We can always stand up for what is right, but in a kind way.

～

MARCH 5

St. John Joseph of the Cross

St. John Joseph of the Cross was born in southern Italy on the feast of the Assumption. He was a young noble, but dressed like a poor man. He did that because he wanted to be as poor as Jesus was.

At the age of sixteen, John Joseph entered the Franciscan Order. He made many sacrifices. He slept only three hours every night and ate very plain food.

Later he became a priest and the Superior of the monastery. Still he always insisted on doing the hardest work. He did the kind of duties that no one would ordinarily like to do.

St. John Joseph had a very loving nature. But he did not try to win love for himself. Instead, he showered all his affection on his brethren and was like a father to all.

This good priest loved God so much that even when he was sick, he kept on working. He dearly loved the Blessed Virgin, too, and tried to bring others to love her.

From this saint let us learn not to be selfish. Let us love everyone alike and show our love in words and deeds.

MARCH 6

Sts. Felicitas and Perpetua

Perpetua was a young wife who lived long ago in the early days of the great Roman Empire. Her father was a rich nobleman, so Perpetua had everything she wanted. But she loved Jesus more than anything in this world.

Perpetua's father was a pagan, and he did everything possible to make her give up her Christian faith to save her life. But Perpetua did not give in, no matter how her father cried and begged and threatened her. At last, he fell onto his knees and kissed her hands, calling her "Lady," instead of "daughter." Still Perpetua did not give up her resolution to be loyal to Christ—not even when she was asked to do it for the sake of her little baby.

She and her Christian maid, Felicitas, were condemned to death.

Felicitas was also a young wife, and while she was in prison for her Faith, she became a mother, too. Her little baby was at once adopted by a good Christian woman. Felicitas was happy because now she could die as a martyr.

Perpetua and Felicitas bravely faced martyrdom together, encouraging and helping each other.

The martyrs were so faithful to Christ as to make great sacrifices and to give up their lives for Him. Let us learn from them at least to make cheerfully the little sacrifices that come our way.

༄

March 7

St. Thomas Aquinas

St. Thomas Aquinas was the son of a noble family of Italy. Thomas was very, very intelligent, but he was never proud about it. He knew that his mind was a gift from God.

When he was nineteen, he entered the Dominican Order, even though his family was very much against it. When he was on his way to Paris to study, his angry brothers captured him and kept him a pri-

St. Thomas Aquinas

soner in one of their castles for two years. During that time they did all they could to make him change his mind. They even sent a bad woman to his room to tempt him. But Thomas grabbed a burning brand from the fireplace and chased her away! His sister also came to try to make him give up his vocation. But Thomas spoke so beautifully about the joy of serving God that it was she who changed her mind and decided to give her life to God! At last the Saint was set free.

Because this lovable Saint was chubby and a bit quiet, he was teased and called the "dumb ox" while he was a student. Yet Thomas never grew angry. He just offered it all to Jesus and Mary, whom he loved with all his heart.

St. Thomas wrote so well about God that people all over the world have used his books for hundreds of years now. The secret of his success was that he never began to write anything without first praying.

When traveling to see the Pope, Thomas became ill. Just before he died, a brother asked him what was the best way of living without offending God. Thomas answered, "He who lives in the presence of God and loves Him will never be separated from Him by sin."

If we want to do well in school, let us imitate St. Thomas by praying and trying our very best.

St. John of God

St. John was born in Portugal. His parents were poor, but very pious. John was a shepherd for a while, then a soldier, and then a storekeeper. All this time he led a bad life. His friendship with sinful men had made him lose his fear of offending God.

When he was forty, a sermon he heard made him feel very sorry for the life he was living. He promised to make up for it. He sold the little that he had and gave the money to the poor. Then he began a new life. Day and night he prayed and did hard penances. His great charity led him to give himself as a servant to a poor family sent into exile.

When he was forty-five, John got a house where he could care for the sick who were too poor to go to a hospital. He founded a religious order for the care of the poor. The members are called Brothers of St. John of God.

One night, St. John found a poor man on the streets who seemed half-dead. He carried him to his hospital. There he put him to bed and began to bathe him, as was his custom. But when he reached his feet, how surprised he was to see that the man's feet seemed to be pierced like Our Lord's. John looked up and saw that the poor man was really Jesus Himself! "John," said Our Lord, "everything you do for the poor in My name you do for Me." Then Jesus disappeared and St. John was left with a great joy in his heart.

After ten years of hard work in his hospital, St. John became sick himself. He died on his knees in front of the altar.

St. John of God turned from his bad way of living to lead a holy life because of one sermon he heard and thought much about. We, too, could become better if we thought more about the good things we read.

❧

St. Dominic Savio

St. Dominic Savio was born in Italy in 1842. One day when he was just four, he disappeared and his good mother went looking for him. She found the little fellow in a corner praying with his hands joined and his head bowed. Already he knew all his prayers by heart. At five, he was an altar boy. When he was seven, he received his First Holy Communion. On that solemn day he chose a motto: "Death, but not sin!" And he kept it always.

"A teenager such as Dominic, who bravely struggled to keep his innocence from baptism to the end of his life, is really a saint," said Pope St. Pius X.

Yes, Dominic was an ordinary boy with an extraordinary love for God.

At the age of twelve, Dominic entered the school run by St. John Bosco. Don Bosco examined him first and at the end of the questions, Dominic asked, "What do you think of me?"

"I think you're good material," answered the priest, with a big smile.

"Well, then," said Dominic, "you are a good tailor, so if the material is good, take me and make a new suit out of me for Our Lord!"

Everyone in the school soon saw from the way he prayed that this boy was different. He greatly loved all the boys and even though he was younger, he used to worry about them. He was afraid that they would lose the grace of God by sinning.

One day, a fellow brought a magazine full of bad pictures to school. In a minute, a group of boys had gathered around him to see it. "What's up?" wondered Dominic and he, too, went to look. Just one peek was enough for him. He grabbed the magazine and tore it to pieces! "Poor us!" he cried in the meantime, "Did God give us eyes to look at such things as this? Aren't you ashamed?"

"Oh, we were just looking at these pictures for the fun of it," said one boy.

"Sure, for fun," answered Dominic, "and in the meantime you're preparing yourselves to go to hell!"

"Oh, what's so wrong about looking at these pictures anyway?" another fellow demanded.

Dominic had a ready answer. "If you don't see anything wrong," he said sadly, "this is even worse. It means you're used to looking at shameful things!"

No one said anything after that. They all realized that Dominic was right.

Another time he stopped a terrific stone-throwing fight between two angry boys. Holding up a little crucifix between them, he said, "Before you

St. Dominic Savio

fight, look at this and say, 'Jesus Christ was innocent and He died forgiving His murderers. I am a sinner, and I am going to hurt Him by not forgiving my enemies.' Then you can start—and throw your first stone at me!"

The two boys were so ashamed of themselves that they made up and promised to go to confession, besides.

One day Dominic began to feel sick and was sent home to get better. There he grew worse, instead, and received the last Sacraments. He was only fifteen then but he did not fear death. In fact, he was overjoyed at the thought of going to Heaven. Just before he died, he tried to sit up. "Goodbye," he murmured to his good father. Suddenly his face lit up with a smile of great joy and happiness. "I am seeing such wonderful things!" he exclaimed. Then he spoke no more, for he had gone to Heaven.

Let us make Dominic's motto, "Death, but not sin" our motto, too.

March 10

Forty Martyrs of Sebaste

Under the Emperor Licinius, these martyrs suffered at Sebaste in Armenia. When all the soldiers of their legion were commanded to offer sacrifice to the gods, these forty heroes bravely refused. They said they would willingly die for their country but they would never commit the sin of offering sacrifice to false gods. In punishment, they were stripped of their clothes and lowered into a little pond. It was winter time and very cold. They were to be left there all night to freeze to death. "It will be a terrible night," they exclaimed, "but it will win us a happy eternity!"

The pagans kept trying to persuade them to give up their faith in the true God. If they would, they could jump into a warm bath prepared nearby. At last, one soldier gave in to the temptation. But no sooner did he enter the warm bath than he died!

A pagan guard had a vision right then of blessed spirits descending from heaven with thirty-nine crowns. He was converted himself, and casting off his clothes, he joined the other thirty-nine. So the number of forty martyrs was complete again, and the Church honors these brave heroes of Christ as saints.

Let us admire the courage of these soldiers and learn from them how to bear without complaining the heat or the cold.

❧

March 11

St. Eulogius of Spain

St. Eulogius belonged to a very famous family of Spain. He was educated by wonderful Christian teachers. While he learned his lessons, he also learned from their example to be virtuous. Even when he grew up, he kept on studying. When he finished he knew many things. He knew much about the Holy Bible. But best of all, he was a man full of a desire to bring God's message to everyone. As a priest, he became himself the head of a famous school. Everyone admired and loved St. Eulogius because he was humble, kind and very close to God.

At this time the Mohammedans were ruling Spain. They were terrible enemies of Christianity. At first they tried to make the people give up their Faith. When the people refused, the Mohammedans began to put them to death.

Eulogius and his Bishop were put in prison along with many other good Christians. In the prison, Eulogius read the Holy Bible out loud all the time to the other prisoners. In this way he filled them with great courage. They did not feel afraid to die for Our Lord. During this time, St. Eulogius also wrote a book encouraging Christians to die rather than give up their holy Faith.

The Saint himself wanted to be a martyr more than anything else. Instead, he was let out of prison. As soon as he was free, St. Eulogius began to preach and he converted many.

The Mohammedans were so angry with Eulogius that they arrested him again. In front of the judge, he bravely declared that Jesus is God. When they condemned him to death, Eulogius thanked God! Very willingly he offered up his life for Jesus.

We are all proud of our country's war heroes, and we dream of doing the great deeds they did.

Let us be very proud of the heroes of our Faith, too, and try to be like them.

St. Gregory the Great

St. Gregory was born in Rome of noble parents. His father was a senator and his mother was a saint, St. Celia. Gregory studied philosophy and while still young, became Governor of Rome.

When his father died, he turned his large house into a monastery. For several years he lived as a good and holy monk. Then Pope Pelagius made him one of the seven deacons of Rome, and when the Pope died, Gregory himself was chosen to take his place. The humble Saint did not want that honor at all. He was so holy and wise, however, that everyone knew he would be a good Pope. Gregory even tried to disguise himself and hide in a cave, but he was found and consecrated Pope, anyway.

For fourteen years he ruled the Church. He was one of the greatest Popes the Church has ever had, even though he always was a sickly man. St. Gregory wrote many books and preached to the people constantly. He cared for people all over the world. Indeed, he considered himself everyone's servant. He was the first Pope to use the title "Servant of the servants of God." Now, all the Popes use this title.

St. Gregory took special, loving care of poor people and strangers. Every day he used to feed them a good dinner. Once the Lord Himself came, dressed like one of the Saint's poor guests. This Jesus did to show St. Gregory how pleased He was with his charity.

Once, when Gregory was still a monk, he saw some blonde boys up for sale in the slave market of Rome. He asked where they were from and was told that they were from England. The Saint felt a great desire to go to England to bring the Faith to those pagans. When he became Pope, one of the first things he did was to send some of his best monks to convert the English to Christ.

The last years of this holy Pope's life were filled with terrible sufferings, yet he continued working for his beloved Church until the very end.

Every morning let us make the resolution to do at least one good deed of charity during the day.

∾

MARCH 13

St. Euphrasia

St. Euphrasia was born of saintly and noble parents. Her father died when she was only five years old. Her mother, who is also named St. Euphrasia, took her to Egypt. There they lived in a large house near a convent of good and holy nuns.

Euphrasia begged her mother to let her serve God in the convent in which the holy nuns lived. Her good mother cried for joy. Soon afterwards, she took the child to the convent and put her in the care of the Abbess. The Abbess asked Euphrasia if she would be able to leave behind all her riches and comforts. She asked the girl if she thought she could live a life of sacrifice for Jesus. The young girl answered right away that she would be happy to do anything, as long as she could stay in the house of God. So the Abbess accepted her.

When her mother died, the Emperor reminded Euphrasia that her parents had promised her in marriage to a rich young senator. Of course Euphrasia wanted to belong to no one but Jesus. So she wrote a respectful letter to the Emperor. In it she said: "I belong to Jesus, and I cannot give myself to anyone else. My only desire is that the world should forget about me completely. I humbly beg Your Majesty to take all the riches my parents left me and give them to the poor. I ask Your Majesty to free all the slaves of my family and to cancel all the debts people owe me."

The Emperor thought her letter was so beautiful that he read it out loud to all the senators. Then he did everything she had asked.

For her generosity, God showered Euphrasia with special favors and graces. On her part, she thought only of becoming a saint. And she succeeded. The devil tempted her very much, especially with temptations of impurity, but Euphrasia prayed harder than ever. She made even more sacrifices than usual. That is why she was always victorious over the devil. She grew holier every day until God called her home to Heaven.

It is all right to be happy with the nice clothes and many good things we have. But we should never forget that all these things are nothing compared to what we shall have in Heaven—if we live as Jesus wants us to live.

St. Matilda

St. Matilda was the daughter of a German count. When she was still quite young, her parents married her to a nobleman named Henry, who became King of Germany.

As Queen, Matilda lived a life of prayer and virtue. Everyone who saw her realized how pure and humble and good she was. She loved to visit and comfort the sick and to help prisoners. Her holy husband saw all the good she was doing, and decided to help her.

When King Henry died, St. Matilda suffered very much. He died very suddenly, and the poor Queen decided then and there to live for God alone. So she called the priest to offer Mass for him and then gave him all the jewels she was wearing. She promised to give up the things of the world from then on.

Although she was a saint, Matilda made a big mistake: she favored her son Henry more than his brother, in the struggle to see who would be king. But she was very sorry for having done this and she made up for it by accepting great sufferings all the rest of her life.

After years spent in practicing charity and penance, St. Matilda died a peaceful, holy death and was buried beside her good husband.

From St. Matilda, let us learn to offer up little sufferings to make up for our sins.

❦

St. Zachary

St. Zachary was a Benedictine monk from Greece who became a Cardinal and then Pope. In his time, there was much fighting all over Italy between one kingdom and another. Pope St. Zachary was the one who kept making peace and saving people from terrible wars. At times he risked his life to do it.

It was because the Saint was so gentle and kind that the leaders did what he asked. Even for his enemies he would do favors and give them the kindest treatment possible. He never took revenge on them.

St. Zachary had special care for the churches of Rome. He loved to make them as beautiful as he could, out of love for Jesus dwelling on the altars.

Towards the poor, this holy Pope was a real father. He built big homes for them and for travellers. His loving heart could not bear to see people suffer. Once he heard that some businessmen had bought poor slaves in Rome and were going to sell them in Africa. He called those men and scolded them for being so cruel. Then he paid them the price they were asking for the slaves and set the poor slaves free.

When St. Zachary died, all the people were saddened to have lost such a good and saintly father.

St. Zachary had much respect for Our Lord's presence in every church. Let us, too, have respect for the House of God and never talk or joke in church.

March 16

St. Abraham

St. Abraham was born in Mesopotamia of a rich, noble family. He married because that was what his parents wanted. But immediately after the wedding, he told his wife that he wanted to live and die as a virgin. Then secretly he left home to live only for God. His friends looked for him for seventeen days. They finally found him praying in a little cell outside the city. He begged them to let him stay and at last they gave in.

Abraham's cell had only one little window, through which he received food and drink. Here he spent all his time adoring and praising God, and begging His mercy. All he had was a cloak and a piece of sackcloth to wear and one dish out of which he ate and drank.

Ten years after Abraham had left the world, he received all his parents' fortune. But he gave it to the poor. Many people called upon him for advice. On seeing this, the Bishop ordained Abraham a priest and sent him to preach to people who were enemies of our holy Faith. Abraham would have been happier to stay in his cell, but he obeyed cheerfully.

He was often beaten and insulted by those people. Three times he was sent away, but each time he returned with greater zeal. After three years, the people were finally moved by his meekness and patience. Through the prayers of Abraham, they all received baptism!

When his brother died, St. Abraham took upon himself the care of his brother's only child, Mary. He placed her in a little cell near his own and instructed her himself. Mary became very pious and dear to God. But after twenty years of this holy life, she was attracted by the world. She ran away to a distant town and there committed many sins. For two years, St. Abraham wept and prayed for her conversion. Finally he found out where she was living, and he went to talk to her. She was so ashamed when she saw him! "Mary," he said, "what has become of your angelic life and your prayers?" Then, seeing how sorry she was, he comforted her lovingly. He promised her that she would be happy again if she would follow his advice. Poor Mary! She cried and thanked him for coming. She promised to obey him perfectly. So Abraham put her on his horse and led her back to her cell. There Mary did great penance and wept for her sins until she died a saint fifteen years later. She was so sorry that she had offended God. And Our Lord showed how pleased He was with Mary's sorrow for her sins. He gave her the gift of working miracles by her prayers.

St. Abraham lived ten more years after he had led his niece, St. Mary, back to God.

St. Abraham converted the pagans and his niece with his prayers and mortifications. We must pray and offer up little sacrifices when we need graces.

༒

MARCH 17

St. Patrick

It is believed that St. Patrick was born in Britain of Roman parents.

When he was sixteen, he was captured by pirates and taken to Ireland. There he was sold as a slave. His owner sent him to tend his flocks on the mountains. St. Patrick had very little food and clothing. Yet every morning, even in rain, snow and ice, he would get up early to pray. A hundred times a day and a hundred times during the night, Patrick prayed to God. His faith thus grew stronger all the time and his love for God increased.

Later, when he escaped from Ireland, he studied to become a priest. But Patrick always felt that he must go back to Ireland to bring that pagan land to Christ. At last his wish came true. He was consecrated a Bishop and sent by the Holy Father to Ireland. How happy he was to bring the good news

St. Patrick

of the true God to the poor pagans of the land where once he had been a slave!

Right from the start, Patrick suffered much. His relatives and friends wanted him to quit before the pagan Irish killed him. Yet the Saint kept on preaching about Jesus, traveling from one village to another. He never rested, and he did great penance for these people whom he so loved. Before he died, the whole nation was Christian! And besides bringing the Irish to the Faith, he made them a civilized, learned people.

Despite such great success, St. Patrick never grew proud. He called himself a poor sinner and gave all the praise to God.

So many of the Irish imitated this holy Apostle that Ireland is called the "Isle of Saints."

Today, we shall perform at least one spiritual work of mercy. For example, we may pray for missionaries in pagan lands.

March 18

St. Cyril of Jerusalem

St. Cyril was born in Jerusalem and at the age of thirty was ordained a priest. He was given the duty of instructing and preparing the people for baptism. Cyril taught in a very clear, simple way that everyone could understand. He often repeated the words of the Holy Bible. Because the words of the Bible are the words of God, they move people's hearts.

When the Bishop died, Cyril was chosen to take his place. Not long after he became Bishop of Jerusalem, a bright cross appeared in the sky. It was two miles long and reached from Mt. Calvary, where Jesus died, to Mt. Olivet, where Jesus suffered the Agony in the Garden. Perhaps this was a sign of the great persecutions the Church had to suffer in this period.

In St. Cyril's time, the Emperor Julian, who had given up his Christian faith, said that Jesus had been wrong when He declared that the temple of Jerusalem would not be rebuilt. He decided to try to prove it. So he spent much money and sent all the materials for a new temple. Many people helped by giving jewels and precious metals. Yet St. Cyril was sure that the temple could not be built, because Jesus, Who is God, said so. And sure enough, first a storm, then an earthquake and finally a fire stopped the Emperor, and those with him had to give up. God had put an end to their wicked plan!

Let us make up our minds never to read or to listen to anything which is different from what Jesus and His holy Church teach us.

❧

MARCH 19

St. Joseph

St. Joseph is a great saint, the foster-father of Jesus Christ, and the husband of the Blessed Mother. He was given the great privilege of taking

St. Joseph

F. Nagni

care of God's own Son, Jesus, and His Mother, Mary. Joseph was poor all his life, even though he came from a family of kings. He had to work very hard in his carpenter shop, but he did not mind. He was happy to work for his little family, the holiest family there ever was.

Whatever the Lord wanted him to do, St. Joseph did at once, no matter how hard it was. He was humble and pure; he was gentle and wise. Jesus and Mary obeyed him perfectly. What an honor for St. Joseph to see the Son of God Himself obeying him and helping him, as a good son!

We pray to St. Joseph as the Patron of the dying, because he had a happy death in the arms of Jesus and Mary.

St. Teresa chose St. Joseph as the protector of her Order of Sisters. She had great trust in his prayers. "Every time I ask St. Joseph for something," she said, "he always obtains it for me."

As Jesus obeyed and helped St. Joseph in his hard and humble work, let us, too, willingly help our parents with the work to be done at home.

MARCH 20

St. Cuthbert

St. Cuthbert lived in England. He was a poor shepherd boy who loved to play games with his friends. He was very good at them, too. One of his friends scolded him for loving to play so much.

Cuthbert never forgot this wise correction. Our Lord granted him a vision when he was fifteen; and after that he strongly desired to become a saint. He entered a monastery and later became a missionary.

From one village to another, from house to house, St. Cuthbert went, on horse or on foot. He did good everywhere, and brought many souls to God. So cheerful and kind was he that everyone felt attracted to him. Yet he himself was more contented to be alone with God.

When Cuthbert was made a Bishop, he worked just as hard as ever to help souls. As he lay dying, he urged his monks to live in peace and charity with everyone.

Let us be so kind and good that no one will find it hard to get along with us.

❧

MARCH 21

St. Benedict

St. Benedict was the son of a rich Italian family. His life was full of adventure and wonderful deeds. As a young boy, he was sent to Rome to study in the public schools. When he was a young man, because he was disgusted with the vices of the world, he left the city and went looking for a place where he could devote all his time to praying and loving God. In a cave in the mountain of Subiaco, he spent three years alone. The devil often tempted him to go back

St. Benedict

to his rich home, but Benedict overcame these temptations by prayer and penance. One day, the devil kept making him think of a beautiful lady he had once seen in Rome. He tried to make him go back to look for that lady. Benedict almost gave in to the temptation, but then he felt so sorry that he threw himself into a bush of long, sharp thorns. He rolled around in those terrible thorns until he was covered with blood. From then on, he had no more temptations to impurity.

After three years, God let a priest know where Benedict was living, and soon many people came to him to learn how to become holy. He became the leader of some men who had asked his help. But when he tried to make them do penance, they grew angry. They were so wicked that they even tried to poison Benedict. He made the Sign of the Cross over the poisoned wine and by a miracle, the glass shattered to pieces! God had saved him!

Later, Benedict became the leader of many good monks.

He founded twelve monasteries in Subiaco, and then went to Cassino, where he built a famous monastery. It was here that St. Benedict wrote the wonderful rules for the Benedictine order. He taught his monks to pray and work hard, and, especially, to be humble always. Both Benedict and his monks greatly helped the people of their times by teaching them how to read and write, how to farm, and how to work at different trades.

St. Benedict was able to do so much good, because he prayed very much.

Whenever we are tempted, especially to impurity, let us say a prayer at once. And let us make whatever sacrifice must be made to avoid sinning.

St. Catherine of Sweden

St. Catherine was born in Sweden of holy parents. Her mother was St. Bridget and her father, the good Prince Ulfo. When she was seven, Catherine was placed in a convent to be educated.

At the age of fourteen, she was given in marriage to a good young nobleman. So well did Catherine speak of the happiness of belonging to God alone that her husband agreed to live with her as her brother. These two holy servants of God spent most of their time in prayer, mortification and works of charity.

St. Catherine had to suffer insults and unkind treatment, even from her own relatives. Yet, she did not become upset. She offered it all to God.

When St. Catherine accompanied her mother to Rome, she received news of her husband's death in Sweden. Many people wanted her to marry again, because she was still young and pretty. But Catherine firmly refused. With the help of God, she remained a virgin all her life.

Four hours a day Catherine prayed. She spent the rest of her time serving God and doing good to many people. After her mother died, she entered a convent. St. Catherine had the great joy of seeing her own mother canonized as a saint.

Let us learn from this pure virgin never to look at anything impure or displeasing to God.

༺

MARCH 23

St. Toribio

This Spanish saint was a famous judge, wise and just. Although he was not a priest at that time, he was asked to become Archbishop of Lima in Peru, South America. That was because everyone knew what a fine Christian he was. Toribio did not think he was worthy. He begged to be excused from the honor. But when he learned about the miserable condition of the Indians in Peru, he could not refuse to help them and to bring them the Faith. He was ordained a priest and set out for Peru.

As Archbishop, St. Toribio traveled all over the land, over the snowy mountains on foot, over the hot sands of the seashore. He built churches and hospitals. He built schools to train priests. He learned the different languages of the Indians so that he could preach to them and hear their confessions. He helped them in their troubles and protected them from being treated cruelly by those who had conquered them.

After a life of charity to his beloved Indians, St. Toribio was called to Heaven.

Let us treat everyone in the same kind manner, and be especially good to those who are not as fortunate as we.

St. Gabriel, Archangel

Gabriel is one of the three glorious Archangels, whom we honor and to whom we pray.

It was St. Gabriel who appeared to the Blessed Mother and told her she was to be the mother of God. God chose him for this very special mission.

In the Holy Bible we read of his appearances on earth. In each of his visits to men, St. Gabriel gives us wonderful examples of charity and humility. He came to tell the Prophet Daniel when Jesus would be born, and he spoke to him with great courtesy and kindness. When he appeared to Zachary to tell him he was to be the father of St. John the Baptist, he showed his humility. He did not even say who he was until just before he disappeared.

And when Gabriel announced to the Blessed Virgin Mary that she was to be the Mother of God, he was very respectful and reverent. With loving devotion, he greeted her and gave her God's message. What great joy it was for him to announce to the Queen of Heaven and earth the coming of Jesus!

Devoutly and respectfully we will say three Hail Mary's to the Blessed Mother every morning and night.

St. Gabriel, Archangel

MARCH 25

Annunciation of the
Blessed Virgin Mary

When the time came for Our Savior to come down from Heaven, God sent St. Gabriel to the little town of Nazareth, where the Blessed Virgin Mary lived. The glorious Archangel entered Mary's little house and found her praying.

"Hail Mary, full of grace!" said the Angel. "The Lord is with you, and you are blessed among women." Mary was surprised to hear the angel's words of praise.

"Do not be afraid, Mary," said St. Gabriel. Then he told her that she was to be the Mother of Jesus, our Savior. Mary understood what a great honor God was giving her. Yet she said, "Behold the handmaid of the Lord!" At that very moment, she became the Mother of God. And still she called herself His handmaid—His servant!

Mary knew, too, that as the Mother of Jesus, she would have many sorrows. She knew she would have to suffer when her Son suffered. Yet, with all her heart, she said, "Be it done to me according to your word."

On this occasion, our Blessed Mother gave us a wonderful example of humility and obedience. Let us, too, show God our love by obeying those who represent Him—our parents and teachers.

134

St. Ludger

St. Ludger was born in Northern Europe. Since his parents were nobles, he was given a very good education. When he was just fourteen, he asked his parents to send him to the great monastery school of Utrecht. There he saw St. Boniface and always treasured the memory of this great Saint. Another Saint named Gregory was his teacher and he found Ludger a very attentive and eager pupil.

After he had studied hard many years, he was made a priest. Now Ludger began to travel far and wide preaching to the people. He was very happy to share all that he had learned about God with everyone who listened to him. Many pagans were converted. Many Christians began to live much better lives. And St. Ludger built churches and monasteries everywhere.

Ludger worked very hard and made much progress. Then, suddenly the Saxons, a group of barbarians, attacked his land and drove all the priests out! It seemed as though all the Saint's work would be lost. But Ludger did not give up. He first found a safe place for his disciples and then went to Rome to ask the Holy Father what he should do.

For over three years, Ludger lived in the Benedictine monastery as a good, holy monk. But he did not forget his poor people at home. As soon as he could get back into his country, Ludger returned

St. Ludger

and continued his work. He labored very hard and converted many of the pagan Saxons.

When he was made a bishop, Ludger gave even more good example by his great kindness and piety. Once, jealous men spoke against him to King Charlemagne, and the King ordered him to come to court to defend himself. Ludger went obediently. The next day when the King sent for him, Ludger said he would come as soon as he had finished his prayers. King Charlemagne was very angry at first. But St. Ludger explained that although he had great respect for the King, he knew that God came first. "Your Majesty will not be angry with me," he said, "for you yourself have told me always to put God first." At such a wise answer, the King realized that Ludger was very holy and from then on, he admired and loved him very much.

St. Ludger died on Passion Sunday. He performed his duties in the service of God even on the day he died.

Let us appreciate the good education our parents are giving us. Some day we will be happy to be able to use all that we have learned.

St. John Damascene

St. John was born in the city of Damascus of a good Christian family. When his father died, he became the Governor of Damascus. At this time, the Emperor Leo made a law forbidding Christians to have statues or pictures of Our Lord and the Saints. St. John Damascene knew the Emperor was wrong and he joined with many others to defend this practice of the Christians. The Pope himself asked John to keep telling people that it is a good thing to have statues and holy pictures. They make us think of Our Lord, our Blessed Mother and the Saints. But the Emperor would not give in to the Holy Father, and he again forbade statues to be put in public places. St. John bravely wrote three letters, telling the Emperor to give up his wrong ideas.

The Emperor became so furious that he wanted revenge. The Saint was condemned to have his right hand cut off, but the Blessed Mother attached it to his arm again in answer to his prayer.

This miracle made John decide to resign as Governor, give away all his money to the poor and become a monk. He kept on writing marvellous books to defend the Catholic religion, and at the same time he did all kinds of humble work in the monastery. One day he even went to sell baskets in the streets of Damascus. Many of those who had known him before were mean enough to laugh at him. Here was the man who had once been the great Governor of the city now selling baskets that nobody wanted to buy! Imagine how St. John must have suffered! Yet he thought of Jesus, the Son of God, Who wanted to be born in a stable, and then he felt happy to imitate Our Lord's humility.

At the end of a long life full of merits, St. John died a peaceful, happy death.

Do we have nice pictures or statues of Our Lord, the Blessed Mother, and the Saints? Let us look at them often. They will remind us to pray to them and to ask their help.

MARCH 28

St. John Capistrano

St. John Capistrano was born in Italy. He was a lawyer and Governor of the city of Perugia. When enemies of the city threw John into prison, he started to think about what he was doing with his life. In the meantime, his wife died. John began to realize that the only thing that really mattered was to save his soul. So when he was set free by a miracle, he entered the Franciscan monastery. He was thirty years old at the time. He did much penance. For many years he ate no meat at all, except when he was sick. He slept only three or four hours at night and his bed was a hard board.

After he was made a priest, John was sent out to preach. He and St. Bernardine of Siena spread

St. John Capistrano

devotion to the Holy Name of Jesus everywhere. John preached all over Europe for forty years, and all who heard his sermons were moved to love and serve Our Lord better.

The greatest moment in the life of this Saint came at the tremendous battle of Belgrade. The Turks had made up their minds to conquer all Europe and wipe out the Church of Jesus. The Pope sent St. John to all the Christian Kings of Europe to beg them to unite to fight the mighty Turkish army. The Kings obeyed this poor, barefoot monk who stirred up their love of God and their courage with his fiery words. But even though a big army of Christians came to fight Mohammed II and his Turks, it looked as though they would lose, for the enemy army was much bigger. Then it was that the Saint himself, though he was seventy years old, ran to the front lines and encouraged the men to keep fighting. Holding his crucifix up high, this thin, small old man kept crying, "Victory, Jesus, victory!" And the Christian soldiers felt full of more courage than ever. They fought until the enemy ran away in great fear!

Just one person can do great things, if he is on God's side. Let us make up our mind always to be on Our Lord's side and stand up for what is right.

Sts. Jonas, Barachisius and their Companions

King Sapor of Persia hated the Christians and he persecuted them cruelly. He destroyed their churches and monasteries. Two brothers named Jonas and Barachisius heard of the persecutions and of the many Christians who had been put to death.

They decided to go to help them and to encourage them to remain faithful to Christ. Jonas and Barachisius knew that they, too, might be captured. But that did not stop them. Their hearts were too full of love of others to have room for a thought of themselves.

When at last these holy brothers were taken prisoner, they were told that if they did not worship the sun, and the moon, and fire and water, they would be tortured and put to death. Of course, they refused to worship anything or anyone except the one true God. They had to suffer greatly, but they prayed and kept thinking of how Our Lord suffered for love of them.

Jonas was placed in a frozen pond and left there a whole night. His wicked tormentors came next morning and asked him if he had had a miserable night. St. Jonas answered that it was the most pleasant night he had ever had because he was suffering for Christ! Many other tortures these saints had to endure, but they accepted all of them willingly and finally were put to death. They gladly gave up their lives for Jesus.

When we have some little pain, are we brave enough to offer it up to Jesus in secret? Or do we have to let everyone know how much it hurts us?

March 30

St. John Climacus

St. John was an intelligent teenager who did very well in school. He could have become a famous teacher, but he decided to serve God with his whole heart. He went to a monastery and tried very hard to get rid of his defects. Then he went to live for forty years by himself and spent all his time praying and reading the lives of the saints. At first, St. John was very badly tempted by the devil. The devil is always furious when people decide to give themselves completely to God. John felt all kinds of bad passions trying to make him give in and sin. But he put all his trust in Jesus and prayed harder than ever. So the temptations never made him fall into sin. In fact, he only grew holier. He became so close to God that many heard of his holiness and went to ask him for advice.

God gave St. John a wonderful gift. This was the gift of bringing peace to people who were upset and tempted. Once there came to him a man who was having terrible temptations. He asked St. John to help him and told him how hard it was for him to fight these temptations. St. John invited him to pray with him to God. After they had prayed, peace filled the poor man's soul and he was never again troubled with those temptations.

When the Saint was seventy-four years old, he was chosen Abbot of Mt. Sinai and Superior of all the monks and hermits in the country. Another abbot asked St. John, before his death, to write the rules which he had lived by all his life, so that others could follow his example. With great humility St. John wrote the book called *The Climax of Perfection*. And that is why he is called "Climacus."

It is very wise to keep a good book in our room and read from it a little bit each day.

∾

MARCH 31

Blessed Amadeus

Amadeus was Duke of the region called Savoy in Italy. He grew up in a palace where many people were leading worldly lives, but he kept himself good. His secret for avoiding sin was to receive the sacraments often, to pray and read good books, especially the Gospel. Even after Amadeus became the ruler himself, he always began his day by reading a holy book. He especially loved to think about the sufferings of Jesus. Then he would assist at Holy Mass so devoutly that everyone who saw him felt a desire to be close to God, too. Next he would take care of all the matters that a ruler has to decide upon. He was so just and fair and kind that no king anywhere was loved more than Amadeus.

The Saint and his holy wife, Yolanda, found great happiness in making others happy. Amadeus often went himself to serve the poor people with his own hands. He said that he enjoyed that more than anything else.

Once he was told that he should not give so much away to the poor. Instead he ought to use that money to build forts to protect his lands. Do you know what Duke Amadeus answered to that? He said: "The best forts are the loving hearts of my people."

Though kind and gentle, on the battlefield Amadeus showed himself a very brave soldier. And he was a good father, raising his children to love and obey God.

The best way to get our younger brothers and sisters to obey us is to win their love. And they will love us if we are always kind and fair with them.

❧

April 1

St. Hugh of Grenoble

St. Hugh was born in France. He grew to be tall and handsome, gentle and courteous, but very shy. Although he always wanted to go off to live alone for God, he was so intelligent that he was given important positions. After he was ordained a priest, he was made a canon of the Cathedral of Valance, and next was chosen Bishop of Grenoble.

As Bishop, Hugh began at once to correct evil ways of living practiced by many people of his diocese. He made wise plans, but that was not all he did. To draw God's mercy down upon his people, St. Hugh prayed with his whole heart and did hard penances. In a short time, his wicked people became very virtuous and pious.

But still Hugh wanted to be a monk. He resigned as bishop and entered a monastery. There he was so fervent in all that he did, and so humble, too, that he became a perfect model of every virtue. Yet it was not God's will for Hugh to be a monk. After one year, the Pope commanded him to become the Bishop of Grenoble again. Right away, St. Hugh obeyed. He knew it was more important to please God than to please himself.

146

For forty years, the good Bishop was sick nearly all the time. Yet he forced himself to keep working, because he wanted to do his duty. He suffered from terrible temptations, too. But he fought them and prayed and never gave in to sin.

When the will of our parents and teachers is different from what we would like, we will drop our plans at once and obey.

April 2

St. Francis of Paola

St. Francis was born in the tiny village of Paola in Italy. His parents were poor but very humble and holy. They had prayed to St. Francis of Assisi for a son, and when he was born, they named him Francis in honor of the great Saint of Assisi. The boy went to a school taught by the Franciscan priests and there he grew in knowledge and virtue.

When he was fifteen, with his parents' permission, he went off to live in a cave, because he wanted to serve God alone. When he was twenty, other young men joined him. Out of charity, St. Francis left his cave and built a church and a monastery for them. He called this new order of religious the "Minims." "Minims" means "the least of all."

Everyone loved St. Francis. He prayed for them all and worked many miracles. He always told his followers that they must be kind and humble, and

147

St. Francis of Paola

do much penance. He himself was the best example of humility and charity. Once someone visited the Saint and insulted him to his face. When he was finished, Francis quietly picked up some hot coals from the fireplace and closed his hands tightly around them without being burned at all! "Come, warm yourself," he said to his accuser kindly. "You are shivering because you need a little charity." At such a miracle, the visitor changed his mind about Francis. From then on, he admired him greatly.

The King of France, who had not lived a very good life, called for St. Francis when he was dying. Just the thought of dying made him shake with fear! He wanted Francis to work a miracle to cure him, but the Saint told him he had come to prepare him to die a holy death. The King had a change of heart and accepted God's will. He died in the arms of the Saint, after preparing his soul well.

St. Francis died at the age of ninety-one. He spent the last three months of his life alone preparing to appear before Jesus, since he knew when he was going to die.

God loves and blesses those who are humble. Let us not show off or look for praise.

❧

April 3

St. Richard of Chichester

St. Richard was born in England. He and his brother were left orphans when Richard was very young. His brother owned some farms and Richard gave up his studies to help him save them from going to ruin. He did so well that his grateful brother wanted to give the farms to him, but Richard did not accept them. He also refused to marry, because he wanted to study. He went to Oxford University, and when he was thirty-eight, he was appointed chancellor of that University. Later, St. Edmund, who was Archbishop of Canterbury, made him Chancellor of his diocese. When St. Edmund died, St. Richard went to the monastery of the Dominican Friars in France and was ordained a priest.

He was consecrated Bishop of Chichester, England, and that is why he is called Richard of Chichester. The King at this time was not very good. Because he wanted someone else to be bishop of Chichester, he made St. Richard suffer much. Yet the good Saint always helped those who offended him. He must have often remembered the words of Jesus: "Love your enemy."

As bishop, St. Richard did his duties well. He was always charitable and kind to sinners who were sorry. However, when he had to be stern, he was. He was not afraid of what might happen to him.

When St. Richard became ill, he foretold his death, because God had let him know the exact place and time when he would die. Many miracles took place at the Saint's grave.

As a farmer, as a chancellor, as a priest and bishop, St. Richard did everything well. We shall try our very best to do our work at home and at school as well as we can, for the love of Jesus.

St. Benedict the Moor

St. Benedict's forefathers were brought in chains from Africa to Sicily. His parents were Negro slaves on a farm. Benedict spent his youth working on this farm.

When he was eighteen, Benedict was given his freedom. He always helped the poor with whatever money he had. This led the people to call him "il Santo Moro"—the Holy Negro.

But there were also jealous people who made fun of Benedict. They insulted him because his parents had been slaves. One day, a holy man was passing by and heard these men insulting Benedict. Turning to them, he said: "You make fun of this poor black man, but before long he will be famous."

Soon Benedict joined a group of hermits and was so virtuous that they chose him as their leader. When the Pope advised all hermits to join monasteries, Benedict became a Franciscan brother. He was made the cook in his monastery, but he also went out to visit sick people and prisoners. He comforted everyone in trouble and worked many miracles for the people of the surrounding villages.

When he was elected Superior, he guided the Community for three years with great wisdom, even though he could not read or write. They wanted to reelect him, but Benedict was so humble that he said he was not fit to remain in such a high office.

His brothers had to give in to his humble request, so they made him Assistant Superior. He was asked to teach all the young men who joined the community how to become good Franciscans. Even though he could not even read, Benedict could explain the Bible and the catechism in a wonderful way, because of his great love for God.

After several years, Benedict asked if he might become cook again. When he was given permission, he went peacefully and happily back to his kitchen. There he spent the rest of his life, serving others with works of charity and prayer.

Let us remind ourselves that if so many became saints, we can become saints, too. It is up to us! To become saints, we do not need to have special qualities. So let us start now.

∾

April 5

St. Vincent Ferrer

A most wonderful Christian hero of Spain was St. Vincent Ferrer. He had a special devotion to the Blessed Mother. Whenever anyone spoke of her, it made him very happy.

When he was eighteen, Vincent entered the Order of St. Dominic. He was a very intelligent man, but because he was also very humble, he never boasted about his intelligence. He was not interested in learning a lot of useless things. After he finished his studies, he read nothing for three years but the Holy Bible, and he knew it by heart.

First Vincent taught at different colleges. Then he became a great preacher. For twenty years he preached all through Spain and France. Many people were converted by listening to him. Among them were Moslems, pagans and heretics. Although there were no microphones in those days, his voice could be heard from a great distance. Everywhere he went, orphanages and hospitals were established, but Vincent remained as humble as ever.

St. Vincent counted on God to make his preaching successful. That is why he prayed before every sermon. But one time, when he knew that a very important person was going to listen to him, he worked harder than usual on his sermon and did not pray. This sermon which he had prepared so carefully did not affect the nobleman much at all. God let that happen to teach Vincent not to count on himself. Another time, this same important person came to listen to the Saint preach, but the Saint did not know it. He prayed and counted on God, as usual. This time the nobleman was greatly impressed by what he heard. When Vincent was told, he said: "In the first sermon it was Vincent who preached. In the second sermon, it was Jesus Christ."

Let us never brag about our good marks or any other success that comes our way. God will keep helping us all our lives if we pray to Him and not count only on ourselves.

St. William the Abbot

William was a young boy of Paris who was taught by his good uncle, the Abbot Hugo. When it was time for him to decide what he should become, William prayed to God to help him make the right choice. Then, on his uncle's advice, he made up his mind to become a priest.

Although William wanted only to do good to everyone, there were some who became his enemies. They were living bad lives, and every time they saw how kind and pure and devout William was, it made them realize how sinful they were. Instead of changing and copying his good example, they tried to get rid of him. They even told the bishop lies so that he would not make William a priest. But the bishop knew what a holy man William really was and he paid no attention to the false accusations. Next his enemies tried to have the Saint sent away, but again God did not let their plan work out. In the end, it was these evil men who were sent away— and by the Pope himself!

St. William and three companions were asked to go to Denmark to convert sinners and pagans and make the Religious there more fervent. The Saint and his companions got a good start, but then everything began to go wrong. They could hardly stand the bitter cold weather and they were very, very poor. Besides that, they did not understand the language, and they had many enemies. Frightened, St. William's three friends gave up and went home to France. But the Saint remained. To show how pleased He was with St. William's trust in Him, Our Lord rewarded him with the conversion of all he had come to help. Then for thirty years the holy Abbot lived in peace and fervor with a great many good monks who imitated his virtues and love of God.

When things get hard, let us not be quitters. God always helps those who turn to Him for help.

❧

April 7

Blessed Herman Joseph

Herman's parents were very poor people who lived in Germany. Because he was so poor, little Herman did not receive much of an education. Yet his great love for our Blessed Mother kept him out of trouble. He grew up under Our Lady's loving care and he went to her every time he needed something. He liked nothing better than to spend time praying to Mary.

When he entered a monastery, Herman was not too happy at first. This was because he had to work in the kitchen and serve his brothers at table. So much of his time was spent with the pots and pans that poor Herman could not pray to his Blessed Mother for hours any more. One day he complained about it to her and Our Lady came to tell him not to worry. "For every day of work," she said, "you earn

Blessed Herman Joseph

a greater reward in Heaven than if you had prayed all day long!" Then Herman was happy. He knew that we please Our Lord and His Mother most when we do our duty in obedience.

Herman received his other name of Joseph in an unusual way. It was given him by the other monks when they saw how much he was like the great St. Joseph, Our Lady's Spouse. Herman was so humble that he did not think he deserved that name. So our Blessed Mother herself came to tell him to keep this name—Herman Joseph.

After he became a priest, the holy monk celebrated Mass with such love of God that people cried to see him. Even though he was so spiritual, Herman worked, too. In fact, he was a good mechanic, and went to one monastery of his Order after another to repair clocks. Herman suffered much from sickness and temptations, but he offered it all to Our Lord and never lost his courage.

Our good actions are like letters that need the right address. This means that they will reach God and bring us a reward only if we do them for Him.

April 8

St. Julie Billiart

Mary Rose Julie Billiart was a strong, young girl of Belgium. In school, her delight was in studying her catechism. In fact, when she was just seven, she used to explain it to other children less intelligent than she. When her parents became poor, she worked very hard to help support the family. She even went to help with the harvesting in the fields. Yet she always found time to visit the sick, to pray, and to teach the catechism.

However, while she was still a young woman, she became very ill and completely paralyzed. Although helpless, St. Julie offered her prayers for the saving of many souls. She was more united to God than ever and she kept on teaching catechism from her sickbed. She gave spiritual advice to everyone who visited her and encouraged all to receive Holy Communion often. Many young girls were inspired by her love for God. So they spent their time and money for good works. With Julie as their leader, they founded the Sisters of Notre Dame de Namur.

Once when a priest gave a mission in the town where Julie was, he asked her to make a novena with him for an intention which he would not tell her. After five days, on the feast of the Sacred Heart, the priest said to her: "Mother, if you have faith, take one step in honor of the Sacred Heart of Jesus." Mother Billiart, who had been paralyzed for twenty-two years, stood up and was cured!

St. Julie spent the rest of her life training young girls to become sisters and watching over her Congregation. She had to suffer much from those who did not understand her mission, but she always trusted in God. Her favorite words were: "How good is the good God!" He assured her that someday her Congregation of Sisters of Notre Dame de Namur would be very large.

And that is just what happened. Today there are a great many of St. Julie's Sisters teaching young girls all over the world.

When something is worrying us, such as a test in school or troubles at home, let us often say: "Sacred Heart of Jesus, I trust in Thee!"

∼∽

April 9

St. Waldetrudis

Waldetrudis was born in Belgium. Her mother, her father and her sister are all saints. She grew up to be a beautiful girl whose sweet ways, even when she was enjoying herself, filled everyone with good thoughts. Many great noblemen wanted to marry Waldetrudis. The one her holy parents chose for her was the Count Meldegario. They could not have picked a better man, because he, too, became a saint!

The holy couple had four boys. And all four of them also became saints. That makes nine saints in one family. Of course, Waldetrudis was very happy that God had given her such a good family. Yet she had to suffer very much in her lifetime.

Jealous ladies spread terrible stories about her. They were not pure and kind as she was, and they did not want people to think she was better than they. So they said she only prayed and did good deeds to hide her secret sins. Of course it was all a lie, but the Saint did not defend herself. She thought of how Jesus suffered on the Cross and like Him, she forgave her enemies. This suffering made her realize how much better it would be to give herself entirely to God as a nun. Her good husband had already gone to become a monk.

Waldetrudis became a holy, pious nun who did much penance and works of charity. For a while she had a great temptation to go back to her home in the world. She felt lonely and sad. But she kept praying and she refused to let the devil's temptation scare her. At last, the temptation left her, and her heart was full of joy again.

Only those who fight hard battles will succeed. If we want to be saints, we must pray and bravely battle against all temptations and difficulties.

APRIL 10

St. Bademus

Bademus was a very wealthy man of Persia who felt the desire to give himself to God. He founded a monastery near his own city and ruled it with great holiness. He spent whole nights in prayer and sometimes, for several days, the only thing he ate was bread and water. He showed his followers how to become saints by being kind, understanding, and loving. In doing these things, Bademus found true happiness.

For thirty-six years, the King had been persecuting the Christians. Now, some of his men arrested the Abbot Bademus and seven of his followers. They were locked up in chains and put in prison for four months. Every day they were taken out and were beaten with ropes and whip-like sticks. With patience and joy they suffered it all for Jesus.

At the same time, a Christian prince named Nersan was also put in prison for the Faith. At first he refused to adore the sun, but then he lost courage and gave up the Faith. The cruel king told Nersan that if he would kill St. Bademus, he would be set free and given back all his property. Nersan picked up the sword to murder Bademus who stood there unafraid to die for Christ. Suddenly Nersan stopped, frightened at the terrible sin he was about to commit. "Unhappy Nersan," said St. Bademus. "I am ready to die, but I wish you were not the one to put me to death!"

Yet Nersan was too much of a coward to stand up and die for his faith. At last he began to strike the Abbot. His hand shook so much that he kept wounding the Saint without killing him. St. Bademus took the terrible pain patiently. At last Nersan killed him. For his crime, he got no reward. A short while after, he himself was tortured and killed by the sword.

Let us resolve never to be cowards who sin out of fear.

APRIL 11

St. Leo the Great

St. Leo was a Roman. At the death of Pope Sixtus, he became Pope.

Those were hard times for the Church because there were barbarian armies attacking Christians in many places and there were many people spreading errors about the Faith. But St. Leo was one of the greatest Popes there ever was. He was absolutely unafraid of anything or anyone. He had great trust in the help of the first Pope, St. Peter the Apostle.

To stop the spread of the false teachings, St. Leo explained the true Faith with his famous writings. He called a council to condemn the wrong doctrines. Those who would not give up their heresy were put out of the Church. Those who were sorry, the Saint received back into the Church and asked people to pray with him for them.

When a great army of barbarians called Huns came to attack the city of Rome, all the people were filled with fear. They knew that the Huns had already burned many cities. To save Rome, St. Leo rode out to meet the terrible enemy leader, Attila. The only weapon he had was his great trust in God! When they met, something wonderful happened. Attila, the cruel pagan leader, showed the Pope great honor, and made a treaty of peace with him. Attila said afterwards that he had seen two mighty figures standing by the Pope while he spoke! These were the great Apostles Peter and Paul, sent by God to protect Pope Leo and the Christians.

Because of his humility and charity, Pope Leo was loved by all. He was Pope for twenty-one years.

We will pray more often for our Holy Father and the Church all over the world.

St. Sabas the Goth

A tribe of barbarians called Goths had come down into Europe and conquered many lands. Some of the Goths became Christians, and one of these was St. Sabas.

From the time he joined the Church as a young boy, he grew in goodness and humility.

The King of the Goths began a terrible persecution of all the Christians among his subjects. Although Sabas made no secret of his Christian faith, he was not taken prisoner during the first year of the persecution. The next year, the King's men came to St. Sabas' town looking for Christians. Some of the people of the town decided to swear that there were no Christians there. But St. Sabas would not stand for that. Without fear he stepped up to the officers and said, "Let no man swear for me. I am a Christian."

The persecutors asked the people how rich St. Sabas was. When they found out that he was just a poor, simple fellow, they did not think it worthwhile to bother with him, so they let him go.

The third year, the persecution of the Christians was worse than ever. This time St. Sabas was taken and tortured in different ways. At last he was thrown into a river and held down with a pole until he died.

Just before he was put to death, St. Sabas joyfully said to the soldiers, "I see what you cannot see. There are people on the other side of the river ready to receive me into the glory of Heaven."

When we find it hard to do our duty, let us think of the reward God will give us.

⮃

April 13

St. Hermenegild

St. Hermenegild was the son of the King of Spain. He himself was a king, because his father had given him a part of his kingdom to govern. Like his father, he believed in the false doctrines called Arianism. But he married a very holy Catholic and through her example, he, too, became a Catholic.

Hermenegild's father was very angry. He wrote to his son: "Remember that I am your father and your king. I command you to go back to the Arian religion. I will be merciful if you obey. If not, I will send an army to attack your kingdom and there will be no mercy for you." He even told Hermenegild that he would take his property, his wife and his

St. Hermenegild

children from him if he did not give up the Catholic Faith.

Hermenegild knew that he could not sin to please his father. So he told him that he was very grateful for all that the king had given him and that he would always respect and love him. But, he said, "I am ready to give up my crown and even my life rather than give up my Faith." Then this holy young king prepared to defend himself against his father.

All the Catholics united under Hermenegild's flag, and they fought bravely. But his father's army was much stronger, and after two years, Hermenegild was defeated. His father promised him that if he would come to ask his forgiveness, he would forgive him. He said that now Hermenegild would not have to give up his Catholic Faith.

The Saint believed his father, and went to kneel at his feet. His father kissed him many times and repeated his promises. But as soon as he had him in his power, he locked him in chains and had him cruelly tortured. Still Hermenegild would not give up his Faith. In fact, in all these sufferings, he grew closer and closer to God. In great anger, his father sent soldiers to murder him.

Hermenegild was declared a martyr and later honored as a saint.

Let us love and respect our parents. But if we are ever commanded anything against the law of God, let us remember that first we must obey God, and then our parents.

St. Justin

St. Justin was born in Palestine. His father brought him up as a pagan. When he was a boy, he read poetry, history, and science. As he grew up, he kept on studying, but for one purpose only. He was looking for the truth about God.

One day as he was walking along the shore of the sea, Justin met an old man. They began to talk together and since he looked troubled, the old man asked him what kind of doubts he had. Justin answered that he was unhappy because he had not found anything certain about God in all the books he had read. The old man told him about Our Lord Jesus Christ and encouraged him to pray so that he would be able to understand the truth about God.

St. Justin began to pray and to read the word of God in the Bible, which he grew to love very much. He was also impressed on seeing how bravely the martyrs were dying for the Christian faith.

After learning more about the Christian religion, Justin became a Christian himself. Then he used his great knowledge to explain and defend the Faith with many writings.

It was in Rome that St. Justin was arrested for being a Christian. The judge asked him, "Do you think that by dying you will enter Heaven and be rewarded?" "I don't just think," the Saint answered. "I am sure!" And he died a martyr.

167

To keep our faith strong, let us make an Act of Faith often. A very short Act of Faith we might repeat from time to time is: "My God, I believe in You."

❦

St. Lydwina

Lydwina means "suffering" and this Saint from Holland spent her whole life suffering for Jesus. As a young teenager of fifteen, she dedicated herself completely to God. Since she was very pretty, she was afraid many young men would want to marry her. So Lydwina asked Jesus to take away her beauty, and He answered her prayer.

One day she went skating with her friends and one of them bumped into her by accident. Lydwina fell hard onto the ice, and that was the beginning of her life of suffering. The pain in her side hurt her so much that she could not stand or sit or lay down. She would ask to be moved from one bed to another, but the pain only grew worse. Crying, Lydwina finally threw herself on her father's knee, saying she could not stand the pain anymore. But more and more pains came—sores on her face, on her body, blindness in one eye, and at last, she could not even leave her bed at all.

For thirty-eight years, Lydwina suffered. At first she felt very bad, but when a priest told her to think of what Jesus suffered, Lydwina took courage. God comforted her so much that she was brave enough to add more penance herself!

Lydwina was good to everyone who came to her poor little room. It became like a little heaven of happiness. She had a way of winning even hard-hearted people and of stopping folks from quarreling.

Lydwina's special love was for Jesus in the Holy Eucharist. For many years, she seemed to live only on Holy Communion.

A strong soldier of Christ can hold back tears and offer his pain to God.

St. Benedict Joseph Labre

This French saint led a most unusual life. He was the son of a store owner and was taught by his uncle, a priest. When the good priest died, Benedict tried to enter a monastery, but was told he was too young. Then he entered another, but his superiors had to dismiss him because he had become like a shadow on account of his poor health. "God's will be done," said Benedict.

While he was gaining back his health, he felt inspired to leave his relatives and his country to live a life of penance in the midst of the world. As a pilgrim, he would travel to the famous shrines of Europe.

Benedict went visiting one church after another. He dressed in rags, with a crucifix over his heart and a rosary around his neck. He slept on the bare

St. Benedict Joseph Labre

ground. The only food he had was what kind people gave him. If people gave him money, he gave it to the poor. In a sack he carried his own Gospel, and medals and holy books to give to others. St. Benedict paid no attention to the beautiful sights in the cities he visited. His only interest was in the churches where Jesus dwells in the Blessed Sacrament.

While he prayed in front of the altar, Benedict was so still and devout that he seemed like an angel adoring God. His white, tired face would glow with happiness. He had a great love for our Blessed Mother, too. "Mary, O my Mother!" he would exclaim.

St. Benedict was not interested in taking care of himself. His only thought was to keep Jesus company in church.

When he died at the age of thirty-five, the fame of this poor holy man spread far and wide.

We cannot imitate the poverty of Jesus in the way St. Benedict Joseph did, but we can imitate this Saint's love for the Blessed Sacrament. Let us go to church often to visit Jesus and to have a heart-to-heart talk with Him. Jesus is our best Friend.

∽

April 17

St. Stephen Harding

Stephen was a rich young Englishman who always looked cheerful and calm. He was a good student and learned much about literature but especially about how to pray well. Once Stephen and a friend set out for Rome as pious pilgrims. They walked along in silence, thinking about God and praying to themselves. They only spoke when they prayed together.

When they returned, Stephen joined a very poor and holy community of monks. Their abbot was another saint, St. Robert. For a while he served God joyfully, but then the monks in that monastery did not want to live such a hard life any more. So St. Robert and St. Stephen, with twenty other fervent monks, went to start a new monastery in a wilderness in France called Citeaux. Here they lived a life of work and great poverty—to imitate the poverty of Jesus. They kept silence very strictly and were very devout and humble.

When St. Stephen became Superior, he had many troubles. There was so little food that he was forced to go out and beg from door to door. Then over half of the monks fell sick and died. It looked as though the community would come to an end, but St. Stephen prayed with faith. And his prayer was rewarded. God sent to this Cistercian monastery the great St. Bernard with thirty other gentlemen.

When he lay dying, St. Stephen heard those around him whispering that he had nothing to fear. Had he not led a virtuous life of hard labor and love of God? But St. Stephen told them that he was afraid he had not been good enough. That shows us how humble this great saint was.

We cannot get to Heaven only by praying. We have to work, too. That means we have to do every one of our duties without being lazy.

Blessed Mary of the Incarnation

Beautiful Barbara Acarie was a French girl who was married when she was seventeen. God sent her six children, and her home was a happy one. She was a very good wife and mother. All her children, her husband, and her servants, too, learned from her a great love for prayer and works of charity.

Once, when her husband was accused of a crime, Barbara herself saved him. She went to court, and all alone proved that he was not guilty.

Although she was so busy with her own family, she always found time to feed starving people, to teach heretics about the faith, to help the sick and the dying, and to encourage sinners to change their ways.

When her husband died, Barbara entered the Carmelite Order. Her three daughters were Carmelites, too. Barbara's new name as a sister was Sister Mary of the Incarnation. She joyfully worked in the kitchen among the pots and pans. When her own daughter became a superior, Blessed Mary willingly obeyed her. So humble was she that as she was dying, she said: "The Lord forgive me the bad ex-

173

ample I have given." But the truth was that she had only done good all her life.

God gives everyone the grace to become a saint in his state in life. Let us, then, pray so that we will do in life what God wants us to do.

᜔

St. Alphege

Alphege is an English saint. He became a monk and after a few years was made abbot of the monastery. When he was thirty years old, he became Bishop of Winchester. He had not wanted this honor, but he accepted it because it was God's will. And he did much good. He was so kind to the poor that there were no beggars left in his whole diocese. Next he was made Archbishop of Canterbury, the most important Church in all England.

The year after he came to the city, a group of fierce raiders, called the Danes, attacked. They burned the buildings and killed many people, even women and children. St. Alphege tried to make them stop, but the cruel raiders took him prisoner and carried him off. They told the people of Canterbury that they would have to pay a large amount of money if they wanted to have their Archbishop back.

St. Alphege would not let his poor Christian people pay that much money for him. He said, "It is better to give what we have to the poor than to take from them the little they have."

174

When the Saint had been in prison seven months, the men who had captured him became drunk one night. Angry because they had not gotten the money they wanted, they took the holy Archbishop and beat him. Then they stoned him. At last, one killed him with an axe.

Like Our Lord, St. Alphege prayed for his murderers just before he died.

Even in prison St. Alphege did not want people to think of him or sacrifice for him. Let us remember that what we suffer silently for God gains a great reward in Heaven for us.

APRIL 20

St. Agnes of Montepulciano

This young saint was born of wealthy parents near the city of Montepulciano in Italy.

When she was just nine years old, she begged her mother and father to let her enter a convent. Agnes was very happy living with the sisters, and before too long she was so good a nun that the other sisters were very pleased to have her. She was of good example to all, especially because of the wonderful way she prayed.

When she was only fifteen, Agnes was chosen superior of a whole convent of nuns! The Pope had to give a special permission to let such a young girl be the head of a convent.

St. Agnes of Montepulciano

Agnes was a very good superior because she was much wiser than most teenagers are. Besides that, she did great penance and was always very sweet and charitable. She truly loved God and her neighbor. God was especially pleased with Agnes and gave her many graces in answer to her prayers. Once He even let her hold the Christ Child in her arms!

Agnes was a sickly woman, but she bore her sickness for years with heroic patience. She never complained or felt sorry for herself. Instead, she offered everything to God.

Towards the end of her life, when her sisters saw that she was not going to get better, they were very sad. "If you loved me, you would be glad," said Agnes, "because I am going to enter the glory of Jesus." She died while she was praying very fervently.

We must always trust that our Heavenly Father will hear our prayers and give us whatever is for our best.

∼∾

April 21

St. Anselm

Anselm was born in northern Italy. From his home, you can see the high mountains called the Alps. When Anselm learned from his mother that God is in Heaven, he loved to look up at the very tops of those mountains. Since he was a little boy then, he thought that the mountains were like ladders leading up to the palace of the King of Heaven.

When Anselm was fifteen, he tried to enter a monastery, but his father was against it. Then Anselm became sick and not long after he got better, his mother died. He was still young and rich and clever, and soon he forgot about wanting to serve God. He began to think only of having good times.

Yet, after a while, Anselm became bored with this way of life. He wanted something better, something more important. So he went to visit the holy Abbot Lanfranc of the great monastery of Bec. He became Lanfranc's very close friend and the holy abbot brought him close to God. He also helped Anselm decide to become a monk.

Three years later, Anselm was made the superior. He was a very warm-hearted man who loved his brother monks dearly. Even those who were jealous of him at first became his friends. When he had to leave them to become Archbishop of the great diocese of Canterbury in England, he told them that they would always live in his heart.

The people of England loved and respected Anselm very much. However, the king at this time was the wicked William Rufus. This king persecuted the Saint in every way and even forbade him to go to Rome to ask the Pope's advice. But Anselm went anyway, and stayed with the Pope until the king died. Then he went back to his diocese in England.

Even in the midst of his many duties, St. Anselm always found time to write important books of philosophy and theology. To please his monks, he also wrote down the many wonderful instructions he had given them about God. He used to say:

"Would you like to know the secret of being happy in the monastery? Forget the world and be happy to forget it. The monastery is a real Heaven on earth for those who live only for Jesus."

Let us realize that just having a lot of fun will not make us happy. True happiness can only be found in loving God and in helping our neighbor.

Sts. Soter and Caius

St. Soter was Pope long ago, in the times of the Roman Emperors. He was a real father to all Christians. He gave much help to those who were poor. He took special care of those who had been condemned to work in dangerous mines because they would not give up their faith. These brave Christians had little to eat and were not allowed to rest hardly at all. Other Christians were chained in prisons. Good Pope Soter did everything he possibly could to comfort and help them.

St. Soter also helped churches that were far away from Rome. This holy Pope was a great preacher. All the Christians loved to listen to him explain our religion, because he spoke so beautifully. He inspired them with new courage to die for Christ rather than sacrifice to false gods. After ten years as Pope, St. Soter himself gave his life for Jesus.

St. Caius was Pope about one hundred years later. He, too, lived in times of persecution and he did all he could to prepare his good people to keep the Faith at any sacrifice. In order to be of more help to his people, he lived eight years in underground rooms, called catacombs. These were cemeteries where the Christians often met in secret to pray and receive the Sacraments. This was their hiding place from the cruel pagan soldiers, who would kill them if they caught them.

St. Caius was Pope for twelve years. Then, he, too, was put to death for the Faith.

Today people in different parts of the world are persecuted because they are good Christians. Let us offer our prayers and sacrifices that they may keep up their courage.

༚

St. George

Pictures of St. George usually show him killing a dragon to rescue a beautiful lady. The dragon stands for wickedness. The lady stands for God's holy truth. St. George was a brave martyr who was victorious over the devil.

He was a soldier in the army of the Roman Emperor Diocletian, and he was one of the Emperor's favorite soldiers. Now Diocletian was a pagan and a bitter enemy of the Christians. He put to death every Christian he could find. George was a brave Christian, a real soldier of Christ. Without fear, he went to the Emperor and sternly scolded him for being so cruel. Then he gave up his position in the

180

Roman army. For this he was tortured in many terrible ways and finally beheaded.

So boldly daring and so cheerful was St. George in declaring his Faith and in dying for it that Christians felt courage when they heard about it. Many songs and poems were written about this martyr. Soldiers, especially, have always been devoted to him.

We all have some "dragon" we have to conquer. It might be pride or anger or laziness or greediness or something else. Let us make sure we fight against these "dragons," with God's help. Then we can call ourselves real soldiers of Christ.

April 24

St. Fidelis of Sigmaringen

This Saint's name was Mark Rey. He was born in Germany and went to the famous University of Freiburg to become a lawyer. Even as a young student, he liked to visit the sick and the poor and to spend many hours praying. His brother became a Capuchin priest, but Mark finished his studies and became a famous lawyer.

Many times he would help poor people who had no money to pay a lawyer. For this reason, he was given the nickname, "The Poor Man's Lawyer."

Because he was very honest and polite, Mark became disgusted with the arguments and dishonesty of those law courts. He decided to become a Capuchin priest. He received the holy robe of the monks and took the name, Fidelis, which means "faithful."

Father Fidelis was filled with joy when he was told to go to Switzerland to preach. In Switzerland there were many enemies of the Catholic faith, and he wanted to try to win these people back to Jesus. His preaching brought wonderful results, and many people were converted. The bitterest enemies grew wild with anger at his success.

St. Fidelis knew that his life was in danger, yet he went right on preaching. In the middle of one sermon, a shot was fired at him, but the bullet missed. He started back over the road on which he had come to the town. A group of men with guns stopped him and ordered him to give up the Catholic religion. The Saint answered meekly but firmly, "I will not renounce the Catholic faith!" At once, the cruel men struck him down.

St. Fidelis pulled himself up and kneeling, prayed: "Lord, forgive my enemies. They do not know what they are doing. Lord Jesus, have mercy on me! Holy Mary, my Mother, help me!" Another blow hit him and then more and more blows until this hero's life was taken away.

It is a great honor to be able to help others come back to Jesus, back to Church. Let us try, by prayer, good example and kind words, to be real apostles.

St. Mark the Evangelist

Mark lived in Palestine at the time of Our Lord. He was a relative of St. Barnabas. While still a young man, he went with the great Apostles Paul and Barnabas on a missionary journey to bring the teachings of Christ to new lands. Before it was over, though, he grew discouraged and went back home to Jerusalem. Later, he was much braver, and he became a beloved disciple of St. Peter, the first Pope. With St. Peter, he went to Rome. Here St. Peter preached about Jesus to the Romans. The people asked St. Mark to write down everything St. Peter said, and he did. This book is called the Gospel of St. Mark.

It is a life of Christ told by St. Peter himself and it gives us many little details that are not in the other Gospels.

Mark was consecrated a bishop and sent to Egypt. There he converted many people. After a life of sufferings serenely endured for the glory of God, he went through a long and very painful martyrdom.

His wicked enemies tied his feet with rope and dragged him through the streets for a whole day. The ground was stained with St. Mark's blood, but he was happy for the chance to suffer for Jesus. That night in prison, Jesus Himself came to comfort and strengthen St. Mark. The next day his enemies

F. Nagni

St. Mark the Evangelist

dragged him on the ground again until he died of his many wounds.

St. Mark's relics were later brought to Venice and today they are venerated in the beautiful Basilica of St. Mark.

There is no book in the world more important than the Holy Gospels. The wisest and holiest of men have always loved to read them over and over again. Let us, too, make sure we have a copy of the Holy Gospels and that we read them.

Our Lady of Good Counsel

Good Counsel means "good advice." The beautiful devotion of Our Lady of Good Counsel goes way back to the year 1467. Even before then, Christians had prayed to our Blessed Mother for her help and advice when they were in doubt. But devotion to Our Lady of Good Counsel really spread everywhere when on April 25, 1467, a most beautiful picture of her appeared in the old Church of Santa Maria at Genazzano, Italy. It was a small picture but the wonderful thing about it was that it stayed right in mid-air, without being held up by anything! At once people began to come from all over to visit the Church of Santa Maria.

Many miracles happened and are still happening at this shrine of Mary. Bishops and even Popes have had great devotion to Our Lady of Good

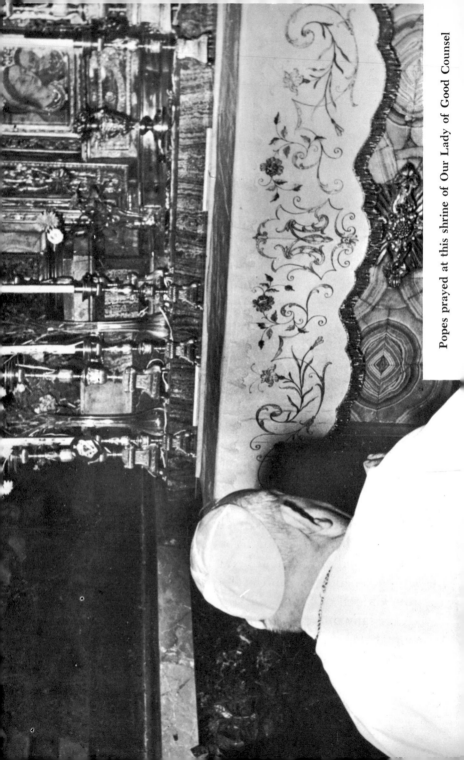

Popes prayed at this shrine of Our Lady of Good Counsel

Counsel. One Pope had her holy picture crowned with gold. There are also many churches named for Our Lady of Good Counsel.

When we have a problem, who can give us better advice than our own good Mother Mary? Let us always pray to Our Lady of Good Counsel to ask her help.

~

St. Peter Canisius

Peter was a Dutchman whose father wanted him to be a lawyer. To please him, young Peter began to study law after he had finished all his other studies. Soon enough, however, he realized that he would never be happy in that life. About that time, people all over were talking about the wonderful preaching of Blessed Peter Faber, who was one of the first members of the Jesuit Order. When Peter Canisius listened to him, he knew he, too, would be happy serving God as a Jesuit. So he entered, and after more years of study and prayer, he was ordained a priest.

The great St. Ignatius soon realized what an obedient and zealous apostle St. Peter Canisius was. He sent him to Germany where Peter labored for forty years.

It would be hard to name all St. Peter Canisius' great works, prayers and sacrifices to save many cities of Germany from heresy and to bring back to the Catholic Church those who had accepted false teachings. It is said that he traveled about twenty thousand miles in thirty years, sometimes on foot and sometimes on horseback.

In spite of all this, St. Peter Canisius still found time to write many books on the Faith. He realized how important books are. So he made a campaign to stop bad books from being sold. And he did all he could to spread good books to teach the Faith. The two catechisms St. Peter Canisius wrote were so popular that they were printed over two hundred times and were translated into fifteen languages.

To those who said he worked too hard, St. Peter Canisius would answer, "If you have too much to do, with God's help, you will find time to do it all."

Most of the wrong ideas on our Faith are the result of not knowing enough about it. Let us often take out books from our school or parish library so that we will know our holy Faith well and be able to explain it to others.

April 28

St. Peter Chanel

From the time he was seven, this French boy took care of his father's sheep. Though poor, he was intelligent and loved his Faith, too. One day, a good parish priest met him and thought so much of Peter that he asked his parents if he could educate him. In this priest's little school and later in the seminary, Peter won the admiration of everyone. While he

St. Peter Canisius

was a parish priest, he was so kind to the sick of his parish that many people decided to change their bad lives and return to God.

Because he had a great desire to be a missionary, St. Peter became a Marist. He hoped he would be sent to the pagans far away, and after a few years, his wish came true. He and a group of his brother missionaries were sent to the islands of the South Pacific. Father Peter and one brother were assigned to the island of Futuna. There the people willingly listened to Father Peter preach. "This man loves us," one of the tribesmen said. "And he does what he teaches."

However, the chief of this tribe became jealous of St. Peter's success. When his own son was baptized, he was furious and sent a band of his men to kill the missionary. All Father Peter said as he lay dying was, "It is well with me." Within a short time after his martyrdom, the whole island became Christian.

Jealousy leads people to do many evil things. If we see others doing good, let us thank God for it and try to imitate their good example.

❧

APRIL 29

St. Peter of Verona

As a young boy, this Italian Saint learned of the Catholic Faith, although his parents were not Catholic. So well did he know his religion that no argument could make him change his mind. And so good a Catholic was he that no bad example led him into sin. He was still young when he entered the Dominican Order. St. Dominic himself gave him the holy habit. Later, as a priest, Peter traveled up and down Italy preaching and converting many people. However, before God gave him the grace of martyrdom, He permitted him to suffer very much. In fact, he was falsely accused of having received women into his cell. His Superiors scolded him very strongly for this, but the humble Saint did not defend himself. He was forbidden to preach any more, and he accepted this penance without a word of complaint. Yet deep in his heart, he suffered greatly. One night when he could not sleep, he fell to his knees in front of the crucifix and sobbed, "Jesus, You know I am pure and innocent. Why do You let me suffer like this?" Back came this answer from the crucifix: "And I, Peter, what did I do to deserve My passion and death?" That gave the Saint courage, and soon afterwards, his innocence was proved.

The enemies of the true Faith, too, made St. Peter suffer. They did all they could to stop him from preaching. Yet he continued without fear. At last he was attacked and murdered. Just before he died, he dipped his finger in his own blood and wrote on the ground: "I believe in God." His murderer, a man named Carino, soon repented of his crime. He became a Catholic, joined the Dominican Order, and died a holy death.

When we recite the Apostles' Creed, let us say it with all our heart, and be grateful to God for giving us the same Faith the Saints had.

St. Catherine of Siena

This glorious saint is the Patroness of Italy, her country. She was the youngest child in a family of twenty-five children. Her mother and father wanted her to wear pretty clothes and choose a husband, but Catherine wanted only to become a nun. When she cut off her long, beautiful hair, to make herself unattractive, her family was so angry that they scolded her all day long and made her work like a slave in her own home. At last, however, they let her become a sister.

St. Catherine suffered terrible temptations after, but she always fought them bravely. Once she said to Jesus, "Where were you, Lord, when I had such shameful temptations?" And Jesus answered, "Daughter, I was in your heart and I made you win with my grace."

Jesus often appeared to St. Catherine and talked with her lovingly. One night, when all the people were out on the streets celebrating, He appeared to her praying alone in her room. With Him was His Blessed Mother. She took Catherine's hand and lifted it up to her Son. Jesus put a ring on the Saint's finger and so she became His bride.

In St. Catherine's time, the Church had many troubles, and there were fights going on all over Italy. The Saint wrote letters to Kings and Queens

St. Catherine of Siena

and went herself to beg rulers to make their peace with the Pope and to avoid wars.

Catherine never forgot that Jesus was in her heart—no matter how busy she was. And through her, Jesus converted the sick people she lovingly nursed and the prisoners she visited in jail. The Pope himself accepted Catherine's advice to go back to Rome from France because it was God's will that he govern the Church from Rome. The Pope listened to St. Catherine and went back, because he knew how close she was to God.

Let us offer our whole heart to God so that like St. Catherine, we will discover how wonderful it is to love the Lord.

May 1

Sts. Philip and James

Philip was one of Jesus' first Apostles. Our Lord found him and said, "Follow me." Philip was so happy to be with Jesus that he wanted to share his happiness with his friend, Nathaniel. "We have found Him of whom Moses and the prophets wrote. He is Jesus of Nazareth," he told Nathaniel.

Nathaniel was not at all excited. Nazareth was just a little village, not a big city like Jerusalem. So Nathaniel said, "Can any good come out of Nazareth?" But Philip did not become angry at his friend's answer. He just said, "Come and see." Nathaniel went to see Jesus, and after he had spoken with Him, he, too, became a zealous follower of the Lord.

St. James was also one of the twelve apostles. He was a cousin of Our Lord. After Jesus ascended into Heaven, James became the Bishop of Jerusalem and the people thought so much of him that they called him, "James the Just," which means "James the Holy One." In all his prayers, he kept begging God to forgive the people. Even when the enemies of Jesus were putting him to death for preaching about Our Lord, St. James asked God to pardon them.

195

St. Philip

St. James

It does no good to become angry if others make fun of us. We will win them little by little if we are patient and keep praying.

MAY 2

St. Athanasius

Athanasius was an Egyptian who devoted his life to proving that Jesus is truly God against the Arians who denied it. Even before he was ordained a priest, he had read so many books on the Faith that he easily could point out the mistakes in the false teachings of the Arians.

For forty-six years, he was Archbishop of the great city of Alexandria in Egypt. Four Roman emperors could not make him stop writing his clear and beautiful explanations of our holy Faith. His enemies persecuted him in every way and sent him into exile many times.

Once they were chasing him down the Nile River. "They are catching up to us!" cried the Saint's friends. Athanasius was not worried. "Turn the boat around," he said, "and row towards them." The men from the other boat shouted, "Have you seen Athanasius?" Back came the answer: "You are not far from him!" The enemy boat sped on faster than ever, and the Saint was safe!

Because the people of Alexandria so loved their good Archbishop, who was a real father to them, they saw to it that he spent the last seven years of his life safe with them. The enemies of the true Faith could not harm him, and he died in peace.

Let us never let the teasing or laughter of our companions stop us from doing what is right. God sees us and He will reward us in Heaven for every good act.

◆

MAY 3

St. Philip of Zell

Philip was an Englishman who made a pilgrimage to Rome and was there ordained a priest. Then he went to live in Germany. He made his home in a woods and lived alone, spending his time praying and growing his own food. The little creatures of the forest were very dear to Philip because they were all created by the good God Whom he loved and served. Birds used to perch on his shoulder and eat right out of his hand. Rabbits played about his feet.

People began to come to ask St. Philip's advice. Even the King, the famous King Pepin of the Franks, used to love to talk with this holy priest. They became good friends, and King Pepin learned from St. Philip to trust in God.

Another priest came to live with the Saint, to share his life of prayer and work. Once two thieves stole the oxen used by the Saint and his companion. But in trying to get out of the woods with the two animals, the robbers lost their way. After going around in circles all night, they found themselves in the morning right back in front of St. Philip's hut! They had a change of heart and begged the good priest to forgive them. St. Philip treated them as special guests before sending them on their way. They were so moved by his goodness that from then on they were different men from what they had once been.

After St. Philip died, a monastery and then a church were built where his little hut had been.

Let us often say a special prayer for the conversion of sinners. These prayers are very pleasing to Jesus, Who wants sinners to return to Him and to be saved.

MAY 4

St. Monica

It was in North Africa that this famous mother of St. Augustine was born. She was brought up as a good Christian. Her strong training was a great help to her when she was married to the pagan Patricius. Patricius admired his wife, but he had a terrible temper and made her suffer much. Still Monica never answered back and never complained about him. Instead she prayed for him fervently. At last, before he died, her prayers and her good example converted Patricius and her mother-in-law, also.

St. Monica's joy over the holy way in which her husband had died soon changed to great sorrow when she found out that her son Augustine was living a wicked life. This brilliant young man of nineteen had turned to a false religion and to evil habits. Monica prayed and cried and did much penance for her son. She begged priests to talk to him. Augustine was brilliant, yet very stubborn, and he did not want to give up his sinful life.

But Monica would not give him up, either. When he went to Rome without her, she followed him. At Rome, she found he had become a teacher in Milan. So Monica went to Milan. And all those years, she never stopped praying for him. What love and faith! After thirty years of prayers and tears, her reward came when Augustine was converted. Not only did he become a good Christian, as she had prayed, but also a priest, a bishop, a great writer, and a very famous saint.

We should not become discouraged if our prayers are not answered right away. Like St. Monica, we must keep praying, because Our Lord promised, "Ask and you shall receive."

❧

MAY 5
St. Pius V

This holy Pope's name was Michael Ghisleri. He was born in a little town of Italy of very poor parents. As a boy, he wanted to become a priest, but it seemed as though his great dream would never come true, because he had no money to go to school. One day, two Dominicans came to his home and when they met Michael, they liked him so much that they offered to educate him. And so at the age of fourteen, Michael joined the Dominican Order.

He became a holy priest, and a superior in different Dominican monasteries. Then he was made a bishop, and later a Cardinal. Courageously he defended the teachings of the Church against those who opposed them. And he always lived a holy life of penance, just as he had done in his monastery.

When he was sixty-one, he was chosen Pope and he took the name Pius V. He who had once been a poor shepherd boy was now the Head of the whole Church. Yet he remained as humble as ever. He still wore his white Dominican habit, the same old one he had had. And no one could persuade him to change it.

There were many problems for Pope Pius V to face. He drew strength from the crucifix. Twice a day he meditated on the sufferings and death of Our Lord. Whenever he entered or left his room, he would kiss the feet of Christ on the cross.

At this time the Turks were trying to conquer the whole Christian world, and they had a great navy on the Mediterranean Sea. A Christian force went to battle them at a place called Lepanto, near Greece.

This was one of the greatest sea battles there ever was. From the moment the army set out, the Pope prayed the Rosary almost without stopping. And he had the people do the same.

Thanks to the help of the Blessed Mother, the Christians won a great victory. In gratitude to Our

Lady, St. Pius V established the feast of the Holy Rosary.

If we make it a habit to say a Rosary every day, we will win our Heavenly Mother's special help and protection from evil.

MAY 6

St. John Before the Latin Gate

St. John was the youngest of the Apostles. Jesus loved him with a special love because he was a virgin. He was the only Apostle who stood right near the cross when Our Lord was crucified.

By the year 95, St. John was the only Apostle still alive. All the others had been martyred. He was known and loved by all Christians for his great virtues.

At last, St. John, too, was arrested in the city of Ephesus during the terrible persecution of Christians ordered by the Emperor Domitian. He was taken to Rome and brought before the cruel Emperor. Even though the Saint was so old, the Emperor felt no pity for him. He commanded St. John to be whipped and then thrown into a pot of boiling oil. The Apostle's face lit up with great joy when he heard the order. He wanted with all his heart to suffer for Jesus, Who died for us. And he was anxious to see his beloved Master again in Heaven.

But God worked a miracle to save St. John from the burning oil. It did not hurt him at all; in fact,

St. John the Apostle

when he was taken out, he looked better and stronger than when he was put in!

More furious than ever, the Emperor sent St. John into exile on the island of Patmos.

This St. John was the brother of the Apostle St. James. One day Our Lord had asked them if they could drink the same cup of sufferings He was going to drink. The two Apostles boldly declared they were ready to suffer anything for Him. Then Our Lord told them they would indeed suffer much for His sake. And so it came about, because both of them underwent martyrdom.

Those who keep themselves pure are especially loved and blessed by God.

❧

May 7

St. Stanislaus

St. Stanislaus was born in Poland. His parents had prayed for thirty years for a child, and at his birth, they offered him to God in gratitude. When he grew up, he studied in Paris. After his parents died, he gave all their wealth to the poor. Then he became a priest, and later on he was made a bishop.

As bishop, Stanislaus won the love of all, because of the way he took care of poor people, of widows and orphans. Often he served them himself.

The King of Poland at that time was Boleslaus II. He was so cruel and so impure that all the people were disgusted. Stanislaus first corrected him privately. The king seemed sorry, but soon started again and he committed more shameful sins. The Bishop then had to put him out of the Church. Boleslaus flew into a rage at that. To get revenge, he ordered two of his guards to kill St. Stanislaus. Three times they tried and failed. Then the king himself, in a mad rage, rushed in and murdered St. Stanislaus right in the chapel, as he was saying Mass.

God worked many miracles after his death, and all the people called him a martyr.

When we are corrected for doing wrong, let us accept the correction humbly and let us put into practice the good advice we are given.

MAY 8

St. Peter of Tarentaise

The whole family of this young Frenchman followed him when he became a religious. His father and two brothers became Cistercian monks like him, and his mother and sister became Cistercian nuns. Peter was not quite thirty when he was made superior of a monastery, high up in the mountains. There he opened a shelter for sick people and for the many travelers crossing the mountains. His great joy was to wait on these guests himself.

Much against his desires, St. Peter was next made Archbishop of Tarentaise. He found his diocese in very bad condition, but he worked so hard for thirteen years that his people became fervent and good. Now, everyone loved and admired the Saint and called him a wonder-worker. Humble St. Peter decided he had better go back to being a monk and serve God hidden in a monastery. So one day, to their great sorrow, the people of Tarentaise learned that their beloved Archbishop had disappeared! It was a whole year before he was discovered in a monastery in Switzerland. There he was doing all the hard work as a poor brother. And no one in that monastery ever dreamed that the new brother was really the great Archbishop Peter!

Since it was God's will, back went the Saint to his diocese, to the immense joy of his people. There he stayed the rest of his life, and spent himself for souls, especially for the poor. Twice in freezing weather, he took off his own habit and gave it to poor men, even though he could have frozen to death himself.

The Saints did their best to avoid being admired. Let us imitate them by doing things only for God, not to win praise and admiration.

❦

MAY 9

St. Gregory Nazianzen

Gregory was born in Cappodocia. His parents were Saints: St. Nonna and St. Gregory the Elder. As soon as he was born, his mother took him to church to offer him to God. At the same time, to sanctify his hands, she touched them to the Holy Bible. As soon as he was old enough, he was given the Bible to read and meditate on. Gregory was sent to the best schools and he studied hard.

At the famous school of Athens in Greece, he met a wonderful student, Basil, who became St. Basil! These two very close friends spent years happily studying together. They respected everyone, but they never went with anyone who did not behave as he should. In the midst of many dangers, they kept themselves pure.

Later, they both became priests and then bishops. Gregory was such a wonderful preacher that great crowds, and even heretics and pagans, came to hear him. They clapped loud and long after his speeches, and this he did not like, because, although he was very learned, he was also very humble.

While he was Bishop of Constantinople, Gregory converted many heretics with his sermons. Because of this, the heretics persecuted him and even tried to take away his life. A young man offered to carry out this murder, but at the last minute, he felt great remorse and threw himself at the Saint's feet. With great sorrow he confessed his evil intention. The Saint forgave him at once and won him with his gentleness. This was, in fact, his motto: "Let us show our enemies what we have learned at the feet of Jesus. We must overcome them by gentleness."

Let us do our best never to be the cause of fights or arguments. And let us be kind and patient when others start trouble.

St. Antonino

St. Antonino

Antonino means "little Anthony," and this Italian saint was given the nickname because he was a small fellow. Yet even as a lad, he showed that he had a lot of good sense and will power. When he was fifteen, he asked to join a Dominican monastery, but the Superior thought he was too young and small. "I'll accept you," he said, "when you know *Gratian's Decree* by heart." This book was several hundred pages long! Antonino accepted the challenge, and one year later, he came back. It would be hard to describe the good Superior's amazement when he found that Antonino had memorized the whole decree! Needless to say, he was accepted at once.

The new religious, though just sixteen, continued to surprise everyone by the perfect way in which he lived the life of his Order. As he grew older, he was given one important position after another. Finally, Antonino was made the Archbishop of Florence.

"The father of the poor" was the name given this Saint. He never refused to help anyone. When he had no more money, he would give his clothes, his shoes, his furniture or—his one mule. Many times this mule was sold to help someone, then bought back for him by wealthy citizens, only to be sold once again to help someone else!

Often St. Antonino would say, "A successor of the Apostles should not own anything except the wealth of virtue."

We may not have much money to give, but we can always give good example, a good word, and a helping hand. All this and more comes under the practice of charity.

∿

MAY 11

St. Ignatius of Laconi

Ignatius was the son of a poor farmer in Sardinia. Though he was a sickly boy, he worked hard in the fields to help support the family of eleven. When he was about seventeen, he fell very ill, and promised to become a Franciscan if he should get better. But when the illness left him, his father said, "We did not promise to do anything in a hurry. It's the same whether you keep your promise today or next year." A couple of years later, Ignatius was almost killed when he lost control of his horse. Suddenly, however, the horse stopped and trotted on quietly. Ignatius was convinced, then, that God had saved his life, and he made up his mind to become a religious at once.

Brother Ignatius never had any important position in the Franciscan Order. For fifteen years he worked in the weaving shed of one monastery and then for forty years, until he died at the age of eighty, he was out on the road as a begging friar. Sometimes doors were slammed in his face, sometimes the weather was bad, and always, there were miles and miles to be walked. Yet Ignatius held himself erect, kept calm and cheerful, and did good everywhere he went. He visited the sick, made peace between enemies, converted sinners, and advised people in trouble. He especially loved children, and they loved him as much.

There was one house from which Brother Ignatius never begged anything. The owner was a rich moneylender who made the poor pay back much, much more than they could afford. This man felt humiliated because Ignatius never came to beg from him, and he complained to the Superior of the monastery. The Superior ordered Brother Ignatius to go to that house, because he did not know what kind of man the moneylender was. The Saint obeyed and brought back a large sack of food. It was then that God worked a miracle, for when the sack was emptied, blood dripped out! "This is the blood of the poor," explained the Saint. "That is why I never ask for anything at that house."

The seventh commandment of God is: "Thou shalt not steal." Let us be honest and keep our conscience clean, not only when it is a matter of big things, but even in small things, such as stealing apples from a neighbor's tree or by cheating on a test in school.

May 12

Saints Nereus, Achilleus, Domitilla, and Pancras

Nereus and Achilleus were Roman soldiers. Out of fear, they carried out the cruel commands of the Emperor, until suddenly they gave up this way of life. They were converted to the Christian Faith and left behind them their shields and bloody arrows forever. St. Peter baptized these two new followers of Jesus, who were soon accused of being Christians. Nereus and Achilleus both professed their Faith and were sent into exile. They were tortured again and again, but they absolutely refused to sacrifice to the false gods of the Romans. For this, they were at last beheaded.

Domitilla was a rich Roman girl who had made up her mind to belong only to Jesus. The young man who had hoped to marry her was furious at her decision. He accused her of being a Christian, and she was put in prison. There she suffered much. When she still would not give up her Faith, she was burned to death.

Pancras was a fourteen-year-old boy who left his rich home to go to Rome. There he was baptized by the Pope himself. Not long after that, he was arrested for being a Christian, but he refused to give up the Faith. In fact, with all the courage of a hero, he offered his head to the executioner to be cut off.

Sts. Nereus, Achilleus, and Domitilla

These four young martyrs could have had all the pleasures money can buy. Yet they did not hesitate to give up the joys of the world in order to win the happiness of Heaven, which is much greater and lasts forever.

Let us often think of the happiness which is waiting for us in Heaven. This thought will make it easier to keep God's law all the time.

∾

MAY 13

St. Robert Bellarmine

Robert was born in Italy. As a boy, he was not much interested in playing games. He liked to spend his playtime in repeating to his younger brothers and sisters the sermons he had heard and in explaining the lessons of the catechism to the little farm children of the neighborhood. Once he had made his first Holy Communion, he used to receive Jesus every Sunday.

Robert's father hoped to make a famous gentleman out of his son. For this reason, he wanted him to study many subjects and music and art, too. Whenever a song had words that were not nice, Robert would make up holy words of his own. "My voice is no good for singing things that are not pure," he would say.

It was his great desire to become a Jesuit priest, but his father had quite different plans for him. For a whole year, Robert worked to persuade his father and at last, when he was eighteen, he was permitted to enter the Jesuits. As a young Jesuit, he did very well in his studies and was sent to preach even before he became a priest. When one good woman first saw such a young man, not even a priest yet, going up into the pulpit to preach, she knelt down to pray that he would not become frightened and stop in the middle. When he finished his sermon, she stayed kneeling, but now she was thanking God for the magnificent sermon this brilliant preacher had given!

St. Robert Bellarmine became a famous writer, preacher and teacher. He wrote thirty-one important books. Three hours every day he spent in prayer. Because of his deep knowledge of sacred matters, he was declared a Doctor of the Church. Yet, even when he had become a Cardinal, he considered the catechism so important, that he himself taught it to his household and to the people.

Let us not miss through our own fault even one religion class, and let us make up our minds to get the best marks in this subject.

St. Boniface of Tarsus

The story of this Saint as it comes to us from tradition, shows God's infinite goodness and mercy.

In the city of Rome there lived a very beautiful and rich woman named Aglae. This lady was so anxious to get attention that three times she paid for special entertainments for all the people. The one in charge of her household was a man named Boniface, and Aglae lived in sin with him. He often got drunk, was impure, and committed many other sins. Yet he was very kind to poor people and to needy travelers.

One day Aglae felt sorry for all the offenses the two of them were giving God. She called Boniface and said, "We have forgotten that we shall some day have to appear before the Lord and answer for our sins. I have heard that whoever honors the relics of martyrs will share in their glory. So you go to the East where there is a persecution and bring me back some relics."

Boniface made ready to go. "I will do my best to bring you back some relics," he told Aglae, "but what if my own body should be brought back to you as one of them?" However, she thought he was only joking. Then Boniface set out. On the way, he became a very different man. He began to pray and to do penance, neither eating meat nor drinking wine. To the poor he met he gave away his money.

Boniface went to the city of Tarsus, where the persecution was worse. As soon as he arrived, he went straight to the governor who right then was cruelly torturing about twenty Christians. "Great is the God of the Christians!" cried Boniface. "Pray for me, servants of Christ, that I may join with you in fighting the devil!"

Furious, the Governor ordered his men to torture Boniface in every way. Then he commanded him to be put to death. Just before being beheaded,

216

Boniface asked for a little time in which to pray. Finally his soul passed from this miserable earth to the glory of Heaven. His body was brought back to Rome and Aglae built a church in which it was kept. She herself did penance for fifteen years until she died.

If we have some friend who leads us into sin, we will break off with him or her at once. For the strength to do it, we shall pray and make some mortification.

༄

MAY 15

St. John Baptist de la Salle

This young Frenchman was studying to become a priest when both his parents died. He had to leave the seminary and go home to take care of educating his brothers. But while he was teaching and training them, he kept on studying himself. So it was that they turned out to be fine young men, and John Baptist was ordained a priest.

At that time, the noble people in France lived in great luxury, and the common people were terribly poor and ignorant. St. John Baptist felt very sorry for the children of the poor, and began to open schools for them. To provide teachers, he started the Congregation of the Brothers of the Christian Schools.

Although St. John Baptist also taught the children himself, he spent most of his time training the teaching brothers. For them he wrote a rule of life

St. John Baptist de la Salle

and a book explaining the best way to teach. He was one of the best educators of all time and he believed in teaching in the language of the people, not in Latin, as others did. He grouped the students into classes and made sure they kept silent while the lesson was being explained.

After a while the brothers opened more schools and taught the sons of the working people and nobles, too. Many difficulties faced the new Congregation, but with St. John Baptist's constant prayer and sacrifices, it continued to grow and to spread everywhere.

To please God and to do well in our studies, we shall be quiet during class and listen to the explanation of the lesson.

St. Ubald

When he was only a child, this son of a noble Italian family became an orphan. His uncle, a bishop, took charge of him and gave him a good education. When he finished his schooling, Ubald had the chance to marry any one of a number of lovely noblewomen, but he wanted to dedicate his life to God. He became a priest, and since his virtue was outstanding, the Pope made him bishop of Gubbio, Ubald's own city.

St. Ubald was so mild and patient that he did not seem to mind any insult. Once a workman repairing the city wall damaged his vineyard very much. The Saint gently pointed it out to him. The workman, who probably did not recognize the bishop, shoved him so hard that he fell into a pile of wet cement and got up all covered with it. Yet he said not one word of complaint and went into his house. The city officials were going to punish the man, but Ubald wanted him to be set free and he himself gave him the kiss of peace.

The holy Bishop did indeed love peace, and he had the courage it takes to keep it. Once, when the people of Gubbio were fighting in the streets, he threw himself between the two angry crowds. He seemed unafraid of the swords clashing and the rocks flying. Suddenly he fell to the ground. The people stopped fighting at once, for they thought the Saint had been killed. But he got up and showed them that he was not even hurt. Then all together, the people thanked God for having stopped them from doing each other more harm. Another time, when the Emperor Frederick Barbarossa was going to attack the city, St. Ubald went out on the road to talk to him, and he convinced this bold emperor to leave Gubbio alone.

The Saint also had much to suffer from sicknesses. Yet he never spoke about his pains, and if someone tried to show sorrow over them, he would change the subject at once. Even in his last sickness, he managed to get up to say Mass and give the people his blessing.

Let us learn from St. Ubald never to give in to anger, and to forgive those who may hurt us in any way.

❧

St. Paschal Baylon

Paschal is a Spanish saint. From the time he was seven until he was twenty-four years old, he worked as a shepherd and never had a chance to go to school. Yet he taught himself to read and write, asking everyone he met to help him. This he did so that he could read from religious books.

Paschal was very honest. If any of his sheep damaged someone's crops in any way he would make sure the owner was paid for what was lost.

When he was twenty-four, the shepherd became a Franciscan brother. His companions in the monastery found him to be a kind, humble man who willingly did the most unpleasant and hardest chores. He practiced even more mortifications than the strict rule required so that he could overcome his temptations. Yet he was a gay and happy soul whose great joy was to be with Our Lord in the Blessed Sacrament. He would kneel for hours at a time before the altar without letting his joined hands touch the pew, and he loved to serve one Mass after the other.

Out of some scraps of paper, St. Paschal made himself a little notebook. In it, in nice handwriting, he wrote down some beautiful thoughts and prayers. After he died, a holy Archbishop read some of these

St. Paschal Baylon

and exclaimed, "These simple souls are stealing Heaven from us!"

St. Paschal's other great love was the Blessed Mother. Every day he said as many Rosaries as he could and he wrote beautiful prayers to our Heavenly Mother.

This humble Saint died with the Rosary in his hands just as the bell rang at the consecration of the Mass. The last word on his lips was the holy name of Jesus.

Let us make it a practice never to pass a church without paying a brief visit to Jesus. He lives there for our love and wants to help us in all our needs.

MAY 18

St. Felix of Cantalice

Felix was born of poor Italian farmers, and as a little boy, he used to take his father's cows out to pasture. He became a shepherd next and when he grew stronger, he took a job ploughing a rich man's fields. Felix got into the wonderful habit of letting everything he saw remind him of God's power and goodness. For a while, he thought he might become a hermit, but he finally decided it would be better to join a monastery.

St. Felix was thirty years old when he became a Capuchin brother. He had to beg the Superior to let him enter. The Superior led Felix to a crucifix and asked him, "Can you live your whole life on the cross with Jesus?" The Saint soon proved that he was ready to suffer anything for the love of God. The duty given to Brother Felix was to beg for food for the community. Joyfully he did this hard, humble work daily for forty years in Rome. Even though he was always among people, he never lost the thought of God's presence, and he was so pure that he said he had not once gazed on a woman's face.

So humble was St. Felix that he hid all the penances he performed. When someone noticed that he was walking barefoot, he said, "I can walk faster this way." Although he could not read or write, St. Charles Borromeo and St. Philip Neri used to go to him for advice. Felix often said that he knew only six letters: five red ones and one white one. By the five red ones, he meant the five wounds of Our Lord, as he was very devoted to the Passion of Jesus. By the one white letter, he meant the spotless purity of Mary. Indeed, by studying and copying these six "letters," Felix became a great saint.

A very powerful means to live as the Saints did is to remember that God sees us all the time. If we remember this, we will never do anything displeasing to Him.

∾

MAY 19

St. Celestine V

When the father of this Italian Saint died, his good mother brought up her twelve children well, even though they were very poor. "Oh, if I could only have the joy of seeing one of you become a saint!" she used to say. Once when she asked as usual, "Which one of you is going to become a saint?" little Peter (who was to become Pope Celestine) answered with all his heart, "Me, Mama! I'll become a saint!" And he did.

When he was twenty, Peter became a hermit and spent his days praying and reading the Holy Bible. If he was not praying or reading, he would copy books or do some hard work so that the devil would not find him doing nothing and tempt him. Because other hermits kept coming to him and begging him to guide them, he started a new Order.

Peter was an old monk, eighty-four years of age, when he was made Pope. It came about in a very unusual way. For two years, there had been no Pope, because the Cardinals could not decide whom to choose. St. Peter sent them a message to decide quickly, for God was not pleased at the long delay. Then and there, they chose the holy old hermit himself! Poor Peter wept when he heard the news, but he sorrowfully accepted and took the name Celestine V.

He was Pope only about five months. Because he was so humble and simple, everyone took advantage of him. He could not say "no" to anyone, and soon matters were in great confusion. At last, the Saint decided that he had better give up his position as Pope. He did so and then threw himself at the feet of the Cardinals to ask forgiveness for not having been capable of governing the Church. What an impression his humility made on all of them!

St. Celestine hoped to live in one of his monasteries in peace. But the new Pope thought it would be safer to keep him where wicked people could not take advantage of him. The Saint was put in a cell and died there. Yet he was cheerful and close to God. "You wanted a cell, Peter," he would repeat to himself, "and a cell you have."

St. Celestine loved to live alone, because he wanted to be closely united to Our Lord. Once in a while, let us stop what we are doing for a few seconds and have a heart-to-heart talk with Jesus.

MAY 20

St. Bernardine of Siena

Bernardine was the son of an Italian governor. Before he was seven years old, his father and mother died, but his good aunt brought him up, and his uncle gave him a good education. He grew to be a tall, handsome boy who was so much fun that all his friends loved to be with him. Yet they knew better than to use any impure words when he was around, for he would not stand for it. Twice when an evil man tried to lead him into sin, Bernardine punched him in the face and sent him running with stones flying after him!

The Saint had a special love for the Blessed Mother, and it was she who kept him pure. Even when he was a teenager, he would talk to her in prayer, as a child talks with his mother. For the poor, he felt great pity, and once, when his aunt had no extra food to give a beggar, Bernardine cried, "I'd rather go without food myself than leave that poor man with none!"

Bernardine became a Franciscan priest and soon began his life's work of preaching. At first, his voice was so hoarse and weak that he could not be heard well. He prayed to Our Lady to change it, and it became clear and strong. Before every sermon, Bernardine read the Holy Bible and prayed before the crucifix. Then after he preached, he knelt again before the crucifix to pray for himself and for those who had listened to him.

In those days, bad habits were ruining both young and old people. "How can I save these lost people by myself?" the Saint cried to the Lord. "With what weapons can I fight the devil?" And God answered, "My holy Name will be enough for you." So Bernardine spread devotion to the Holy Name of Jesus. He used this Name a great many times in every sermon and had people put it over the gates of the cities, over their doorways—everywhere. With this devotion and devotion to the Blessed Mother, this great Saint converted thousands of people all over Italy.

Let us invoke the Holy Name of Jesus very often. We will realize how powerful it is against every danger we may face.

MAY 21

St. Andrew Bobola

Andrew was born in Poland, and after he became a Jesuit priest, people began to realize what a great preacher he was. For twenty years, he traveled from one village to the next, converting those who had left the Catholic Church. Then he was made Superior of one of the houses of his Order. A terrible sickness spread through that land, and St. Andrew risked his own life to help the sick and the dying.

After being Superior, he went back to preaching and was so successful that enemies of the Church tried in every way to stop him. For several years, in every village, they trained groups of children to follow him, calling him names and shouting to drown out his voice when he tried to preach. Still the Saint never lost patience with them or quit.

At last, Father Bobola was captured by those who hated him and the Catholic Church. He was beaten without mercy, but he would not give up the Faith. Then they began to torture him in ways too cruel to describe. Because he kept calling on Jesus and Mary, they tore out his tongue. They wounded him in every part of his body. Finally they ended the Saint's life by cutting off his head.

Let us bravely and patiently offer up our small sufferings for the love of Jesus, Who died on the cross for love of us.

St. Andrew Bobola

MAY 22

St. Rita of Cascia

Rita was born in a little Italian village when her good parents had already grown rather old. They had fervently begged God to send them a child, and they brought her up very well. However, when, at fifteen, she asked them to let her enter the convent, they wanted her to marry, instead.

The man they chose for Rita turned out to be a very mean, unfaithful husband. He had such a hot temper that everyone in the neighborhood was afraid of him. Yet, for eighteen years, his wife patiently took all his insults. Her prayers, gentleness and goodness at last won his heart, and he returned to God. In fact, when his temper seemed about to get the best of him, he would leave the house because he did not want to make Rita feel bad, and would return when he calmed down.

The Saint's happiness over her husband's conversion did not last long, for one day he was suddenly murdered. Yet she forgave his murderers and tried to make her two sons forgive them, too. When she saw that they, instead, were determined to revenge their father's death, she prayed, "Lord, I would rather see my sons dead than see them stain their souls with sin." Her courageous prayer was answered. In one year, both boys died, and while she nursed them lovingly, Rita had the grace to persuade them to forgive, and to ask God's forgiveness for themselves.

St. Rita of Cascia

Left alone in the world, the Saint now tried three times to enter the convent in Cascia, but that community was not permitted to accept widows. She did not give up, however, and at last, they made an exception for her. In the convent, Rita was outstanding for her obedience and charity. She had great devotion to Jesus Crucified and once, while praying, she asked Him to let her share some of His pain. One thorn from His crown of thorns pierced her forehead and made a sore that never healed. In fact, it grew so bad and gave off such an odor that St. Rita had to stay away from the other Sisters. She was happy to suffer, and died when she was seventy-six years old.

If we want to convert a person who is far from God, let us pray with faith and without ceasing, until we receive this grace.

❧

MAY 23

St. Julia

St. Julia was born of noble parents in North Africa. When she was still quite young, her city was conquered by barbarians. Julia was captured and sold as a slave to a pagan merchant. But she did not complain or feel sorry for herself. She accepted everything, and performed the most humble tasks with wonderful cheerfulness. For Julia loved God with her whole heart. In her spare time, she read holy books and prayed fervently.

One day her master decided to take her with him to France. On the way, he stopped at an island to go to a pagan festival. Julia refused even to go near the place where they were celebrating. She did not want to have anything to do with those superstitious ceremonies.

The governor of that region was very angry with her for not joining in the pagan feast. "Who is that woman who dares to insult our gods?" he cried. Julia's owner answered that she was a Christian. He said, too, that although he had not been able to make her give up her religion, still she was such a good, faithful servant that he would not know what to do without her.

"I will give you four of my best women slaves for her," offered the governor. But her master refused. "No," he said. "All you own will not buy her. I would willingly lose the most valuable thing in the world rather than lose her."

When the merchant was asleep, however, the wicked governor tried to make Julia sacrifice to the gods. He promised to have her set free if she would. But she absolutely refused. She said she was as free as she wanted to be as long as she could serve Jesus. Then the pagan ruler, in great anger, had her struck on the face and her hair torn from her head. She was next put on a cross to hang there until she died.

We would never look down on anyone if we stopped to think that poor or homely boys or girls may be much closer to God than we are.

St. David I of Scotland

David was the youngest son of St. Margaret, Queen of Scotland and her good husband, King Malcolm. He became king himself when he was about forty. Those who knew him well saw how little he wanted to accept the royal crown. But once he was King, he was a very good one.

St. David ruled his kingdom with great justice. He was very charitable to the poor and let all his subjects come to visit him whenever they desired. He gave everyone good example with his own love of prayer. Under this holy king, the people of Scotland united more closely into one nation and became better Christians.

King David established new dioceses and built many new monasteries. He gave much money to the Church during his rule of about twenty years.

Two days before he died, he received the last Sacraments and spent his time praying with those attending him. The next day, they urged him to rest, but he answered: "Let me think about the things of God, instead, so that my soul may be strengthened on its trip from exile to home." By home, the Saint meant our heavenly home. "When I stand before God's judgment seat, you will not be able to answer for me or defend me," he said. "No one will be able to deliver me from His hand." So he kept on praying right up until he died.

When we are tempted to excuse our faults by saying, "Everyone else does it," let us remember that this excuse will not count when we go before God to be judged. . . .

May 25

St. Gregory VII

This Pope's name was Hildebrand and he was born in Italy. His uncle was the superior of a monastery in Rome and there the young boy was sent to be educated. Later, Hildebrand became a Benedictine monk in France, but soon he was called back to Rome. There he held very important positions under several Popes until he himself was made Pope.

For twenty-five years he had refused to let himself be elected. But when Pope Alexander II died, all the Cardinals made up their minds to elect Hildebrand Pope. With one voice they cried out, "Hildebrand is the elect of St. Peter!" "They carried me to the throne," wrote the Saint afterwards, "and my protests did no good. Fear filled my heart and darkness was all around me."

These were truly dark times for the Catholic Church, because kings and emperors were naming the men they wanted to be Bishops and Cardinals and even Popes. Many of these were not very good men and so they gave bad example. The first thing Pope St. Gregory did was to pray for days. Then he asked others to pray for him, because he knew that

235

without prayer, nothing can be done. Afterwards, he began to act to make the clergy better and to keep the civil rulers out of the affairs of the Church. This was a very difficult work because the rulers were all against any change. However, some gave in. But the Emperor Henry IV of Germany caused Pope Gregory great sufferings. He was a young man, sinful, and greedy for gold. He would not stop trying to run the affairs of the Church, and he even sent his men to capture the Pope. But the people of Rome rescued the Saint from prison, and Gregory put the Emperor out of the Church. Henry set up another man as Pope. Of course this man was not the real Pope, but Henry tired to make people think he was. Then, once again the Emperor sent his armies to capture the Saint. Gregory was obliged to leave Rome. He retired to Salerno, where he died. His last words were, "I have loved justice and hated evil. That is why I am dying in exile."

Let us learn from this great Saint that the first thing to do in our difficulties is to pray.

May 26

St. Philip Neri

This Italian Saint was called *Pippo buono*— "Good little Phil"—when he was a child. He was always so jolly and friendly that everyone he met loved him. He studied in Rome and while still a teenager, gave up a great amount of money he could have received from his uncle. He studied hard and led a pure, good life. Once some evil young men hid two bad women in his room to tempt him to sin. Philip could not go out, but he saved his soul from any impure sin by kneeling down and praying out loud with all his heart. Those women were so struck with shame that they did not even dare to look at the Saint!

When Philip became a priest, he did much good to poor children, to sinners, to sick people, and to all. Because of him, the whole city of Rome became better. He treated himself very strictly, but he was gentle and kind to everyone. He listened to confessions for hours every day. He worked miracles, knew the future, and read minds. But to avoid the admiration of the people, he played jokes and did funny things, like shaving only one side of his face, so that they would laugh and forget how holy he was.

St. Philip cheered up all who came near him. Often he would say: "I will have no scrupulosity and no melancholy in my house." He was always ready to comfort and help everyone. At the same time he was very prudent. Once he was called to a sick woman's bed, but when he got there, he found that she was only pretending to be sick. She wanted to tempt the Saint to sin, instead. St. Philip turned right around and left at once. So pure was he that many times one look of his drove temptations away.

To conquer temptations of impurity, we must avoid the occasions of sin. If we cannot avoid these occasions, let us pray and be modest, and then Our Lord will help us.

St. Bede the Venerable

This English priest is famous not only as a Saint, but also as a writer of history. St. Bede loved the Holy Bible very much. He tells us that it was a joy for him to study the Bible, teach it, and write about it.

When sickness forced him to stay in bed, his pupils came to study by his bedside. He kept on teaching them and working on his translation of St. John's Gospel in English. Many people could not read Latin and he wanted them to be able to read the words of Jesus in their own language. "I do not want my pupils to read false things," he said.

As he grew worse, St. Bede was happy that he was about to go back to God. His brothers in the monastery wept when he told them that they would not see him again on earth. The Saint kept on working, even though he was dying. At last, the boy who was doing the writing for him said, "There is still one sentence, dear Master, which is not written down." "Write it quickly," answered the Saint. When the boy said, "It is finished," the Saint said, "Good! You are right—it is finished. Now hold my head so that I may have the happiness to sit facing the place where I used to pray and there call upon my Heavenly Father." So it was that St. Bede died right after he had sung the "Glory be to the Father."

Let us never lose time. Our Lord will not reward us for bragging, but for the good deeds we do.

St. Augustine of Canterbury

This Italian missionary to England was the Abbot of a monastery in Rome. Pope St. Gregory the Great chose him and forty other monks to go preach the Gospel to the pagans in England. They started out, but when they reached Southern France, people warned them that the English pagans were very fierce. All the monks felt discouraged and asked Augustine to go back to obtain the Pope's permission to give up the whole idea. The Pope, however, said: "Go on, in God's name! The greater your hardships, the greater will be your crown. May the grace of God protect you!"

In England, the missionaries were well received by King Ethelbert, whose wife was a Christian princess from France. They formed a procession when they landed and walked along singing psalms. At their head they carried a cross and a picture of Our Lord. This little army of Christ soon conquered many souls. King Ethelbert himself was baptized, and on Christmas of the same year, ten thousand of his subjects became Christians. Pope St. Gregory was very happy when he heard this news. He sent more priests to England, three of whom became saints.

St. Mary Magdalen dei Pazzi

In his humility, St. Augustine often wrote to ask the Pope the best thing to do in different matters. And St. Gregory gave him much holy advice, too. Speaking about the many miracles St. Augustine worked, the Pope said: "You must rejoice with fear and fear with joy for that gift." He meant that Augustine should be happy that through the miracles the English were being converted. But he should be careful not to become proud.

At Canterbury, St. Augustine built a church and a monastery, which became the most important in England. It was there that he was buried.

When we are commanded something by our parents or superiors, let us try our best to do it, even if it seems difficult, because God will help us.

∾

MAY 29

St. Mary Magdalen dei Pazzi

This Italian Saint was the only daughter of very rich parents. When she was fourteen, she became a boarder at a convent school, and there she grew to love life in a religious house. But about a year later, her father took her home and began to think of choosing a rich husband for her. Her heart, however, was set on becoming a nun, and she told her parents that three years before she had already made a vow of chastity. They could not believe it, but finally they let her enter the Carmelite convent. Only fifteen days later, however, they came and took her home, hoping to make her change her mind. After three months of trying, they gave up and let her go back for good, with their blessing.

As a novice, St. Mary Magdalen fell very sick and was permitted to make her profession ahead of time. Since she was suffering greatly, one of the sisters asked her how she could stand that pain without a word. The Saint pointed to the crucifix and said: "See what the great love of God has suffered for my salvation. This same love sees my weakness and gives me strength."

St. Mary Magdalen had great sufferings her whole life, and she also had very strong temptations to impurity and to greed for food. She overcame everything by her great love for Jesus in the Holy Eucharist and for Mary. Often she ate only bread and water, and practiced other mortifications. Moreover, her love for Jesus became so great that she would say, "Lord, let me suffer or let me die." With tears she would pray and offer her pains for sinners and pagans, right up until she died. She once said: "O my Jesus, if I had a voice loud and strong enough to be heard in every part of the world, I would cry out to make You known and loved by everyone!"

Our love for God and for souls will grow, too, if we look at the crucifix from time to time and think of how much Jesus loved us.

St. Joan of Arc

Joan was born in a little village of France. From her gentle, loving mother, she learned to be a good housekeeper. "I can sew and spin as well as any woman," she once said. She loved to pray, especially at the shrines of our Blessed Mother. This honest, kind little peasant girl was to become a great soldier-saint. One day while she was watching her sheep, St. Michael theArchangel, the patron of her country, told her, "Daughter of God, go save France!" For three years she heard the voices of saints telling her to go, and when she was sixteen, she began her marvellous mission.

At that time there was a war going on between France and England. It was called the Hundred Years' War. England had won so much land that the King of England called himself the King of France, too. The real French King was a weak, fun-loving man who thought the French armies would never be able to save the country.

With his permission, St. Joan led an army into the city of Orleans, which the English had almost captured. In her white, shining armor, this young heroine rode with her banner flying above her. On it were the names of *Jesus* and *Mary*. She was hit by an arrow in the great battle of Orleans, but she kept on urging her men to victory, and at last they won! St. Joan and her army won more and more battles

St. Joan of Arc

and the English armies had to retreat. After these glorious victories, Joan's time of suffering began. She was captured by the enemy, and the ungrateful French king did not even try to save her. She was put in prison and after an unfair trial, was burned at the stake.

Joan was not even twenty, and she had a great horror of fire. Yet she went bravely to her death, and her last word was "Jesus!"

When we meet with difficulties, instead of giving up, let us say this prayer: "By myself I can do nothing, but with God I can do all things."

❧

May 31

St. Angela Merici

Angela was born in a small Italian town and became an orphan at ten. She and her beloved sister were taken care of by their uncle. When she was thirteen, another big sorrow fell upon Angela. The sister she loved so much died suddenly, even before there was time to give her the last Sacraments. Angela was worried about her, but in His goodness, Jesus let her know that her sister was saved. To thank Him, the Saint gave her heart completely to Him.

When she was about twenty-two, she began to realize how little the poor children in her town knew about religion. Their parents were not teaching them anything about it. Angela asked some of her girlfriends to join her in teaching Catechism to these children. None of the girls had money or important positions, but they were anxious to help Angela do good to the children.

At that time there were no Orders of teaching Sisters at all. No one had ever thought of such a thing. St. Angela Merici was the first one to gather together a group of women to open schools for children. At first these women lived in their own homes, and because of many difficulties, it was a very long time before they could live together in a convent. The Saint herself died when her Congregation had just started. But she had great trust in God. She knew He would take care of the mission she had begun. And so He did. Her Congregation, called the Ursuline Sisters, spread to many countries and has become famous for its many good works in the Church of God.

The life of this Saint was one of prayer and patience. Let us not be discouraged even if we cannot do all the good we want to do. God will reward us for trying to do what we can.

JUNE 1

St. Pamphilus

Pamphilus was born in Lebanon and became a famous scholar in his own city. He studied in Egypt and then settled down in Palestine. Here he became a priest and started a school for the study of the Holy Bible.

Pamphilus loved to read and to study religious writings. He collected a wonderful library of them, which was preserved for a long time after he died. He was so anxious to have many people read God's message in the Bible that he would give away his copies of the holy Book. In those days, when there were no printing presses, books cost a great deal of money, because they had to be copied all by hand. Yet St. Pamphilus was so generous that he gave many away.

This Saint treated everyone, even poor slaves, as his brothers. He gave all the money he received from his father to his relatives and friends and to poor people. After working hard all his life, he was put in prison for refusing to worship false gods. He kept on writing the two years he was in prison. Then he and other faithful Christians were beheaded and so won the martyr's crown.

Little by little, let us build up an inspiring home library. Then let us make use of it. We will be sur-

*prised at how good we feel when we read books on
our holy Faith!*

JUNE 2

St. Pothinus and the Martyrs of Lyons

Lyons is a city in France, and back in the very
early days of the Church, there was a great persecution of the Christians in that region. As it grew worse,
some weak Christians were so afraid of being tortured that they gave up their Faith. But the braver
ones, who trusted in God, soon won back their weak-
er brothers, and all together, they suffered for Jesus.

Some were burned with red-hot plates; some
were thrown to beasts; some were whipped; and
some were roasted in an iron chair. A slave girl
named Blandina amazed her persecutors by her courage. She was tortured all day long, but in the end, it
was her torturers who gave up, not she. On the last
day of the martyrdoms, Blandina was brought out
before all the people to suffer again. Yet she looked
as happy as if she were going to her wedding! In
fact, she was so intent on talking in her heart to Jesus
that she did not even feel it when she was tossed
over and over again by a bull! When she was killed,
the pagans themselves said they had never seen a
woman show such courage.

The leader of all these martyrs was the bishop
of Lyons, St. Pothinus. He was ninety years old.
They kicked and beat him so much that he died two
days later in prison.

Let us always be thankful that we share in the divine Faith of these strong Christians. May we never be ashamed of being followers of Christ.

∽

JUNE 3

St. Clotilda

Clotilda was the daughter of the King of Burgundy. After her father's death, her uncle became King, and the princess was brought up in his court. Although this court was full of dangers to her soul, she did not let the attractions of pleasures make her sin. When the pagan King of the Franks, Clovis, asked for her as his wife, her uncle gave permission, but said she must be allowed to practice her Christian Faith.

King Clovis of France was a hot-tempered barbarian, but his Queen Clotilda soon won his heart with her beauty, sweetness, and charming ways. Although she spent many hours in prayer and secretly practiced penance, she dressed and acted as a Queen should, to please her husband. The great desire of her heart was to see him become a Christian.

One day, as he was going into battle, she told him to pray to the God of the Christians. During the battle, King Clovis' soldiers began to go over to the enemy. He saw that he would surely lose, and he vowed that if Clotilda's God would make him victorious, he would become a Christian. He won the battle, and on Christmas Day, Clovis and over three thousand Franks were baptized. It is easy to see why St. Clotilda is called the Apostle of France.

After her husband's death, she had to suffer much from the fighting of her sons, and she tried in every way to keep peace among them. When she was dying, she begged them to treat their subjects well, to protect the poor, and to live in peace. Then she turned all her thoughts to God and prepared herself for death by praying with great devotion.

In the midst of many dangers and in the company of very rough people, Clotilda became a saint. We, too, can become saints if we try to imitate her by praying and being kind all the time.

JUNE 4

St. Francis Caracciolo

This Italian Saint lived like other young noblemen, even though he was a devout Christian and very charitable. He loved all sports, but his favorite was hunting. Then when he was twenty-two, a disease something like leprosy brought him very close to death. While he was sick, he thought about the emptiness of the pleasures of the world and the happiness of those who serve God alone. So he made a vow that if he got better, he would dedicate his life to God. The disease left him so fast that it seemed a miracle, and the young man began his studies to become a priest.

Later, the new priest joined a group who were devoted to caring for prisoners and preparing condemned criminals to die a good death. But his great mission was begun when he and another priest, John Augustine Adorno, started the Congregation of Minor Clerks Regular.

When John Adorno died, Francis was chosen superior, even though he did not want the honor. So humble was he that he used to sign his letters, "Francis the sinner." And he took his turn, like the other priests, in sweeping floors, making beds, and washing dishes. He often spent almost the whole night praying in church, and he wanted all the priests to spend at least one hour a day in prayer before the Blessed Sacrament.

St. Francis spoke so often and so well about God's love for us that he was called, "Preacher of the Love of God." He carefully guarded his purity and converted some evil women who tried to make him sin. Always he practiced mortifications of every kind.

Just before he died, St. Francis suddenly cried, "Let's go!" "Where do you want to go?" asked the priest by his bed. "To Heaven! To Heaven!" came the answer in a clear, happy voice. And right afterwards, the Saint died.

Good times are not enough to fill our hearts. Let us use some of our free time doing something worthwhile so that our life, too, may be useful.

St. Boniface

This great Apostle of Germany was an Englishman. When he was a small boy, some missionaries who were staying at his home talked to him about their work and filled him with a great desire to become like them. While still very young, he entered a monastery school and some years later he himself became a very popular teacher. When he was ordained a priest, he gave many sermons taken from the Bible, which he dearly loved to read.

Boniface daily grew in love for God and for souls. So, with his Superior's permission, he became a missionary to Germany, which at that time covered a large part of Europe. With the blessing of Pope St. Gregory, he preached with wonderful success.

Boniface was a man of great courage. Once, to prove that the pagan gods were false, he did a bold thing. There was a certain huge oak tree that the pagans thought was sacred to their gods. In front of a large crowd, Boniface struck it a few times with an axe. The big tree crashed, and split into four parts. The pagans saw that their gods were false when nothing happened to the Saint for this act.

Everywhere Boniface preached, new members came into the Church. In his lifetime, he converted millions. In place of the statues of the gods, he built churches and monasteries.

When he was seventy-three, St. Boniface left someone else in charge of his work, and sailed with

St. Boniface

some companions to preach to more pagans. Here, too, he was successful and he baptized large numbers. Then, one day, as he was about to give some converts the Sacrament of Confirmation, he was martyred. A group of fierce pagans swooped down on their camp, and the Saint would not let his companions defend him. "Our Lord tells us to repay evil with good," he said. "The day has come for which I have waited so long. Trust in God, and He will save our souls." The barbarians attacked, and Boniface was the first one they killed.

Even today there are millions of souls who do not know the true God. Let us pray for them, and if God inspires us to become missionaries, let us be generous and courageous enough to follow His call.

JUNE 6

St. Norbert

Norbert was a German who was good while a boy and young man. Then at the court of the Emperor, Henry V, he spent nearly all his time in the pleasures of the world, and he thought only of honors, feasts and parties. One day, however, frightened by a flash of lightning, his horse threw him and he was knocked unconscious. When he came to his senses, he was touched by the grace of God, and he made up his mind to lead a better life. Moreover he went back to the idea he once had had—to become a priest, and he did.

Then he worked hard to make others turn from their worldly ways and gave good example by selling all he had to give the money to the poor. St. Norbert also became the founder of a new Congregation for the spreading of the Faith.

Later, he was chosen bishop of the city of Magdeburg. He entered the city wearing very poor clothes and no shoes. The porter at the door of the bishop's house did not know him and refused to let him in. He told him to go join the other beggars! "But he is our bishop!" shouted those who knew the Saint. The porter was amazed and very sorry. "Never mind, dear brother," said St. Norbert kindly, "you judge me more correctly than those who brought me here."

St. Norbert had to combat a heresy which denied that Jesus is really present in the Holy Eucharist. His beautiful words about Our Lord's presence in the Blessed Sacrament brought the people back to their holy Faith.

Let us go to receive Jesus in Holy Communion often—at least once a week. If we feel little love for the things of God, Jesus will make us warm with devotion. If we feel weak in spirit, He will make us strong. If we feel sad, He will console us.

◆

JUNE 7

Blessed Anne Mary Taigi

Anne Mary came from a poor Italian family. Because her father was not a hard-working man, her good mother worked all day long as a servant. To make sure her daughter would grow up to be good, she placed her with the sisters during the day and took her home each evening. She also taught her how to take care of a house and sent her to learn dress-making. The family grew poorer all the time, and Anne Mary's mother decided to let her become maid to the rich woman for whom her father was working.

Anne Mary was very pretty and she began to admire her own good looks. When she was twenty, she met and married a handsome young servant named Dominic Taigi. He was proud of his pretty wife and the two of them thought only of dressing up and having as much fun as they could. After some months, however, Anne Mary felt unhappy over the way she was living and she made up her mind to change. She began to wear plain clothes and to pray much more.

The Taigis had seven children in their forty-eight years of married life. Their home was poor but always neat and peaceful. Although the Saint's hus-band was a rough, stubborn man who easily flew into a rage, Anne Mary was so loving and so good to him that he became a better Christian. She kept her children busy all the time and taught them to be obe-dient. The whole family prayed together and all were happy, even though sickness, suffering and death often caused them sorrow. Anne Mary was always busy in the simple duties of the house, but she kept herself very close to God all the time. Our Lord even gave her the gift of working miracles and telling the future. And sometimes, right in her kitchen, the love of God would burn so strong in her heart that she would have to lean against the wall until she came out of ecstasy.

Though poor herself, Anne Mary offered what she could to the poor. She gave good advice to the many people who came to her, especially young persons. Even bishops and public leaders asked her advice, because they knew she was very dear to God.

Let us say our morning and night prayers every day. During the day, let us do well everything we do, and offer it up to Jesus. In this way we, too, will become saints in whatever life God plans for us.

June 8

St. William of York

William Fitzherbert was born in England and was the nephew of King Stephen. As a young man, he was rather easy-going and even a bit lazy. He was very popular with the people of his city of York, however, and years later, when their archbishop died, he was elected to take his place. In those times princes used to interfere in the election of the bishops. This is why many priests did not think William had been properly chosen, since it was his uncle, the King, who had appointed him. Even the great St. Bernard persuaded the Pope to make someone else Archbishop of York. Poor William! Sent away and humiliated, he went to live with his uncle, a bishop, and would not accept any of the comforts his uncle offered him. He was a very different man now.

The people of York were angry at what had happened and there were fights between them and those who did not want William. But the Saint kept praying for peace for six years, and his prayers were answered. When the other archbishop died, the Pope sent William back to York, to the immense happiness of all the people. But he was an old man by this time, and one month later, he died.

St. William silently suffered all the accusations made against him, even though he did not deserve them. This teaches us to take corrections well.

∾

JUNE 9

St. Columba of Iona

Columba was an Irishman and sometimes he is called by his Irish name of Columkille. He studied at famous monastery schools and became a good poet. Then he became a pupil of St. Finian and later a priest. Before he was twenty-five, he had had the good fortune to study with a number of great Irish saints.

Columba was a tall, strong man with a loud, beautiful voice that people said could be heard a mile away. For fifteen years, he went all over Ireland preaching and starting monasteries. Yet he never stopped studying and he made every effort to obtain many books.

When he was forty-two, St. Columba left Ireland to try to win pagans in Scotland for Christ. On the island of Iona he built a monastery which became very famous. From this monastery, many missionaries to Scotland and England were to come. St. Columba began his mission to Scotland by going to the castle of the pagan King. The King had commanded his soldiers not to let the Saint enter. But when Colomba lifted his arm to make the sign of the cross, the gates fell open by themselves! The King was so amazed that he listened to his words about the Christian Faith and greatly honored St. Columba from then on. Because of the many converts he made, the Saint is called the Apostle of Scotland.

Columba was once a rather rough, quick-tempered man and, though his name means "dove," he was not gentle at all. But he changed so much that he became loving with everyone, serene and full of holy joy.

The saints were not born saints. They had to overcome their defects. Let us, too, see what our greatest defect is and then pray and work hard to correct it.

JUNE 10

St. Margaret of Scotland

Margaret was an English princess. She and her mother sailed to Scotland to escape from the king

St. Margaret of Scotland

who had conquered their land. King Malcolm of Scotland welcomed them and fell in love with the beautiful princess. Margaret and Malcolm were married before too long.

As Queen, Margaret changed her husband and the country for the better. Malcolm was good, but he and his court were very rough. When he saw how wise his beloved wife was, he listened to her good advice. She softened his temper and led him to practice greater virtue. She made the court beautiful and civilized. Soon all the princes had better manners, and the ladies copied her purity and devotion. The King and Queen gave wonderful example to everyone by the way they prayed together and fed crowds of poor people with their own hands. They seemed to have only one desire: to make everyone happy and good.

Margaret was a blessing for all the people of Scotland. Before she came, there was great ignorance and many bad habits among them. Margaret worked hard to obtain good teachers, to correct the evil practices, and to have new churches built. She loved to make these churches beautiful for God's glory, and she embroidered the priest's vestments herself.

God sent this holy Queen six sons and two daughters. She loved them dearly and raised them well. The youngest boy became St. David. But Margaret had sorrows, too. In her last illness, she learned that both her husband and her son, Edward, had been killed in battle. Yet she prayed: "I thank You,

Almighty God, for sending me so great a sorrow to purify me from my sins."

Let us take this saintly queen for our example. While we do our duties, let us keep in mind the joys that God will give us in Heaven.

∾

June 11

St. Barnabas

Even though he was not one of Our Lord's twelve Apostles, Barnabas is called an apostle by St. Luke because he received a special mission from God. He was a Jew and was born on the island of Cyprus. His name was Joseph, but the Apostles changed it to Barnabas, which means "son of consolation."

As soon as he became a Christian, St. Barnabas sold all he owned and gave the money to the Apostles. He was a good, kind-hearted man, full of zeal to win souls for Christ. When he was sent to the city of Antioch to govern the new Christians there, he found that there were to many for only one man to guide. Then, because he was very humble, he asked St. Paul to come to share the government of the Church there with him. He was never interested in keeping honor for himself; he only wanted to give glory to God.

Sometime later, the Holy Spirit said through the prophets at Antioch: "Set apart for Me Paul and Barnabas for the work to which I have called them." Not long afterwards, the two apostles set off on a

St. Barnabas

daring missionary journey. They had many sufferings to bear and often risked their lives, but their preaching won many converts.

Later St. Barnabas went on another missionary journey, this time with his relative, John Mark. They went to St. Barnabas' own country of Cyprus. So many converts did the Saint win there that he is called the Apostle of Cyprus.

When there is some good to be done, let us do it eagerly and only for God's greater glory, not for praise.

St. John of Sahagun

St. John was born at Sahagun, Spain. He received his education from the Benedictine Monks of his town, and then became a parish priest. He could have lived a very comfortable life in the cathedral parish or in other wealthy parishes, but John wanted to imitate Our Lord's poverty. He chose to keep charge only of a small chapel, where he offered Mass, preached, and taught catechism. He began to be very hard on himself and to practice real poverty.

St. John next went to the great University of Salamanca, because he realized that he needed to know theology better. After four years of study, he became famous as a preacher. Nine years later, after a serious but successful operation, he joined a community of Augustinian friars. There he was outstanding for his obedience and humility. His beautiful sermons brought about a change in the people of Salamanca. They were always quarreling violently among themselves and often the young noblemen fought each other in revenge. St. John succeeded in ending a great many of these bitter fights and persuading people to forgive. He was not afraid to correct evils, even when the sinners were important people who might take revenge. Once he corrected a powerful Duke for the way he was making the poor people suffer. In anger, the Duke sent two men to kill St. John. But when these two saw the Saint, so calm and holy, they were struck with sorrow and asked his pardon. Then the Duke fell sick, and through the prayers of St. John, he repented his sins and even got better.

It was the graces he received from prayer and from the Holy Mass that gave St. John his special power as a preacher. He said Mass so devoutly that sometimes he had the great privilege of seeing Jesus at the moment of the Consecration.

This Saint was so calm and inspiring because he was holy. If we keep our conscience clean, we, too, will have peace and be very happy.

∿

June 13

St. Anthony of Padua

This very popular saint was born in Portugal and the name given him at Baptism was Ferdinand.

St. Anthony of Padua

At the age of fifteen, he entered the Augustinian Order and spent all his time in prayer and study.

When he was twenty-five, he heard about some Franciscans who had been martyred by the Moors in Chica. From then on, Ferdinand felt a strong desire to die for Christ. He joined the Franciscans, who had been founded only a little while before, and took the name of Anthony. Then he went off to Africa to preach to the Moors. But he soon became so sick that he had to leave. No one in his new Order knew what a brilliant mind he had, because he kept his talents hidden. So he was sent to a lonely hermitage in Italy, and there he washed pots and pans and did other humble chores.

Our Lord, however, wanted St. Anthony to save many souls by preaching. One day, at a gathering of many priests, it was suddenly discovered that there was no preacher! Anthony was told to get up and give the sermon as best he could. How amazed everyone was when he preached a marvelous sermon, full of wise and holy thoughts! From then on, until he died nine years later, St. Anthony preached all over Italy. He was so popular that people even closed their stores to go to hear him. Often the churches could not hold the crowds and then he would preach out in the open. Heretics, criminals, and sinners of every kind were converted.

Anthony was short and rather plump, but he had such virtue and such a love for sinners that just the sight of him was enough to make many repent and confess their sins.

So many miracles have taken place and so many people have obtained favors by praying to him that St. Anthony is famous as the "Wonder-worker."

The statue of St. Anthony shows him with Baby Jesus. This is because once the Holy Child appeared to the Saint. Other pictures show him holding a Bible because he knew and loved the Word of God very much.

Like St. Anthony, let us love to pray and work unseen. In this way, we shall not become proud, and God will reward every prayer we say and everything we do for love of Him.

❦

JUNE 14

St. Basil the Great

Basil was born in Asia Minor. His grandmother, father, mother, two brothers and a sister are all saints. He was an excellent student and then a teacher, but his sister, St. Macrina, advised him to give up his high place in the world to become a monk. He settled in a wild spot and there founded his first monastery. The rule he gave his monks was so wise that monasteries in the East have followed it down to our own times. Yet Basil himself was called from his monastery to become an archbishop and a great champion of the true Faith against the Arian heretics.

When the Emperor sent one of his officials, a prefect, to make Basil stop preaching against the Arian heresy, he found he could get nowhere with

St. Basil the Great

the Saint. "Are you crazy?" the prefect shouted. "Are you not afraid of the Emperor's anger, or exile, or death?" "No," said St. Basil. "A man who has nothing does not have to be afraid of losing anything. And you cannot exile me, because the whole earth is my home. As for death, it would be a kindness. One blow would end my life and my sufferings together." The prefect could not believe his ears. "Never before has anyone dared to talk to me like this," he said. St. Basil answered, "Perhaps you have not had much to do with Christian bishops!"

The Emperor tried three times to write an order for the exile of the Saint, but each time the pen split in his hand.

Basil always found time to help the poor. He grew very angry with selfish people who refused to give to those in need. "You say you do not have enough for yourselves," he once exclaimed. "Yet while your tongue makes excuses, your hand accuses you. That ring shining on your finger declares you to be a liar!" He wanted poor people themselves to help those worse off. "Give your last loaf to the beggar at your door," he urged, "and trust in God's goodness."

We will never be ashamed of being devout and showing our Faith with such actions as blessing ourselves every time we pass a Catholic Church.

June 15

St. Germaine of Pibrac

Pibrac is the little village in France where Germaine was born and spent her life. She was always a sickly girl and not pretty at all. In fact, her right hand was deformed and helpless. Her father paid little attention to her, and her stepmother did not want her around her own healthy children. So Germaine slept with the sheep in the barn, even in cold weather. She dressed in rags and was laughed at by other children. When she came home at night with the flock of sheep she had tended in the fields, her stepmother often screamed at her and beat her.

Yet this poor girl learned to talk with God and to remember that He was with her all the time. She always managed to get to Mass and she received Holy Communion as often as she could. Her sheep she would leave in care of her Guardian Angel, and never once did one wander away from the staff she planted in the ground.

Germaine often gathered young children around her to teach them their Faith and fill their hearts with God's love. She tried her best to help the poor, too. She shared with beggars the little bit of food she was given to eat. One winter day, her stepmother accused her of stealing bread and chased her with a stick. But what fell from Germaine's apron was not the expected bread. It was summer flowers!

By now people no longer made fun of Germaine. In fact, they loved and admired her. She could have begun to live in her father's house, but she chose to keep on sleeping in the barn. Then, one morning, when she was twenty-two, she was found dead on her straw bed. Her life of great suffering was over and God worked miracles to show that she was a Saint.

The main virtue of this Saint was patience. She carried her big cross well, because she went to Holy Communion often. In our little sufferings, let us turn to Our Lord in Holy Communion and ask His help.

June 16

St. John Francis Regis

When he was eighteen, this French Saint entered the Jesuit Order. In the seminary, his love for God and for souls showed in the way he prayed and in his eagerness to teach catechism in the parishes when he could. After he was ordained a priest, St. John Francis began his work as a missionary preacher. He gave very simple talks that came right from his heart. He especially spoke to the poor, ordinary folks, and they came in great crowds to hear him. He spent his mornings praying, hearing confessions, and preaching. In the afternoon, he would visit prisons and hospitals. To someone who said that the prisoners and bad women he converted would not stay good for long, the Saint answered: "If my efforts stop just one sin from being committed, I shall consider them worthwhile."

Into wild mountain parishes he went in the coldest days of winter to preach his missions. "I have seen him stand all day on a heap of snow at the top of a mountain preaching," said one priest, "and then spend the whole night hearing confessions." Sometimes he would start off for a far-away town at three o'clock in the morning with a few apples in his pocket.

Once, on his way to a village, St. John Francis fell and broke his leg. Yet he kept on going, leaning on a stick and on his companion's shoulder. When he reached the village, he went at once to hear confessions, without letting his leg be treated. At the end of the day, when the doctor looked at it, his leg was found to be completely healed!

St. John Francis died on one of his preaching missions, after falling sick while lost at night in the woods. Just before he died, he exclaimed: "I see Our Lord and His Mother opening Heaven for me!"

God would give us many more blessings and graces if we would forget our own wants and help our parents, family, and friends.

∼✌

June 17

Sts. Teresa and Sanchia

These two sisters were daughters of the King of Portugal. Teresa was the older one. She married

King Alfonso IX of Spain and became the mother of several children. But this marriage was not valid and it was wrong for Teresa to stay as his wife. Because she loved the king dearly, it was very hard for her to leave him. Yet, she did not want to disobey God's law, and finally she went back to Portugal.

On her own land, Teresa built a large convent for Cistercian nuns. She herself shared their life fully, even though she did not stay there all the time, for she had to take care of her other property.

Her sister, St. Sanchia, never married. She, too, founded a convent on her land and devoted herself to good works. When she visited her beloved sister, Teresa, and saw what a holy life the Cistercian nuns led, she changed her convent into a convent of the Cistercian Order and joined it herself. After Sanchia's death, St. Teresa took her body back to her own convent. Then, when she had settled quarrels between her children and the children of King Alfonso's second wife, she took the veil of a nun in her convent. For almost twenty years, she lived as a very fervent sister. When she died, she was buried beside St. Sanchia.

If we ever make a promise to do something wrong, let us make sure we do not keep it. We cannot offend God to please someone else.

JUNE 18

St. Ephrem

Ephrem was born in Mesopotamia. He was not baptized until he was eighteen, but right afterwards he could think of nothing but leading a holy life. The thought of appearing before God after death to be judged made him tremble and he wanted to prepare for that judgment by living well. He was naturally quick to become angry, but he gained such a control over himself that people thought of him as a very calm man.

Ephrem became a hermit in a cave near the city of Edessa in Syria. His clothes were just patched rags and he ate only enough to keep alive. His chief work all this time was the writing of spiritual books. So holy and beautiful are these books that St. Ephrem is given the title of "Doctor of the Church."

He often went to preach in Edessa, and people cried when he spoke about God's judgment. Because he thought he was a great sinner, he wept all his life for the slight sins he had committed as a child. When St. Bazil met him and asked if he were Ephrem, the famous servant of Jesus, St. Ephrem said, "I am Ephrem who walks unworthily on the way of salvation." Then he asked and received from St. Bazil much advice on how to live his spiritual life in the best way possible.

St. Ephrem is also called the "Harp of the Holy Ghost," because he wrote many beautiful hymns. These hymns were very popular and as the people sang them, they learned much about the Faith. In this way, too, Ephrem saved them from falling into heresy.

So humble was this Saint that in his last sickness, he said to his friends: "When I die, treat my body without any respect, in order to show what I am."

We, too, will be judged after our death. But if we think of our judgment now, we will prepare for it with a good life.

≈

JUNE 19

St. Juliana Falconieri

Juliana was the only daughter of a very rich Italian couple. She came in answer to their prayers when they were already growing old. After her father died, her uncle, St. Alexis, helped her mother with her education. St. Alexis was one of the Founders of the Servite Order, the Servants of Mary. Juliana had such a devotion to Our Lady that she decided to become a Servite nun. She and other devout women spent their time in prayer and works of mercy. St. Juliana is considered the Foundress of the nuns of the Servite Order because she wrote their rule of life.

Never did the Saint lose a chance to help someone. She especially worked to make peace between enemies and to win sinners back to Jesus. Though sick herself, she loved to take care of the sick and to make their sufferings easier to bear. In her own sufferings she was always cheerful.

St. Juliana's great love was Jesus in the Holy Eucharist. Her heart was broken when she could not receive Holy Communion because of the stomach disease that led to her death. But Jesus worked an amazing miracle to reward her devotion. As she lay dying, she asked the priest to lay a Host on a linen over her heart. He did and at that moment she died. The Sacred Host disappeared at the same time, and an image of Jesus on the Cross was found on her skin at the spot where the Blessed Sacrament had disappeared.

St. Juliana wanted to receive Jesus in Holy Communion, even when she could not. And we? Do we go to receive Our Lord in Holy Communion as often as possible?

June 20

Blessed Osanna of Mantua

This Italian Saint was the oldest child of a large family. Her father had wanted her to marry, but Osanna gave herself entirely to God.

When she was eighteen, Osanna received a wedding ring from Our Lord. Though no one else could see it, she always felt it on her finger. She also felt some of the sufferings Jesus suffered—the crown of thorns, the wound in His side, and the wounds in

St. Aloysius Gonzaga

His hands and feet. She lived at home and served her family in every way, yet she belonged to the third order of St. Dominic and wore the habit of that order.

Strange as it may seem, Osanna was asked by the Duke of Mantua to run the affairs of his kingdom while he was away. She who had never been to school knew how to make the best decisions because she trusted completely in God. And she used her friendship with the Duke to help everyone in any kind of trouble.

A great many of Blessed Osanna's prayers were for the Church and for Italy. She feared God would send great punishments for the many sins being committed in her time. Yet she was not a gloomy soul. She loved her friends dearly, and people crowded her house to ask her advice and comfort.

A person living in the world can become a saint, if he prays, keeps away from sin and does good deeds. To learn how to live such a holy life, we should read inspiring books.

❧

June 21

St. Aloysius Gonzaga

Aloysius, the Patron of Catholic youth, was the oldest son of an Italian marquis. Since he was so full of life, his father planned to make a great soldier out of him, and when he was only five, he took him to an army camp. There little Aloysius marched in parade and even managed to load and fire a gun one day while the camp was at rest! He learned rough language, too, from the soldiers, but when he found out that this talk was shameful, he felt very bad.

As he grew, Aloysius was sent to the courts of dukes and princes. Many sins of dishonesty, hatred, and impurity were being committed in this high society. But the only effect it all had on the Saint was to make him more careful to protect his purity. He fell sick and that gave him a good excuse to stay in his room to pray and read the lives of the saints.

When Aloysius was sixteen, he resolved to leave the world and become a Jesuit, but his father refused his consent. However, after three years, he finally gave in. Once he had entered, Aloysius begged to serve in the kitchen and to wash dishes, because he wanted to practice humility. He would say, "I am a crooked piece of iron and am come into religion to be made straight by the hammer of mortification and penance."

When a terrible disease broke out in Rome, Aloysius asked to be allowed to care for the sick. He who had always had servants to wait on him gladly washed the sick and made their beds. He served them until he caught the sickness himself.

St. Aloysius was only twenty-four when he died. His last words were, "I am going to Heaven."

The virtue which is outstanding in St. Aloysius is purity. To keep pure we should do what he did, that is, mortify all our senses, and especially our eyes.

St. Alban

St. Alban was the first martyr of England, his own country. During a persecution of Christians, Alban, though a pagan then, hid a priest in his house. The priest made such a great impression on this kind pagan that Alban received instructions and became a Christian himself.

In the meantime, the governor had been told that the priest was hiding in Alban's house, and he sent his soldiers to capture him. But Alban changed clothes with his guest, and gave himself up in his stead. The judge was furious when he found out that the priest had escaped and he said to Alban, "You shall get the punishment he was to get unless you worship the gods." The Saint answered that he would never worship those false gods again. "To what family do you belong?" demanded the judge. "That does not concern you," said Alban. "If you want to know my religion, I am a Christian." Angrily the judge commanded him again to sacrifice to the gods at once. "Your sacrifices are offered to devils," answered the Saint. "They cannot help you or answer your requests. The reward for such sacrifices is the everlasting punishment of Hell."

Since he was getting nowhere, the judge had Alban whipped. Then he commanded him to be beheaded. On the way to the place of execution,

St. Audrey

the soldier who was to kill the Saint was converted himself, and he, too, became a martyr.

Jesus taught us, "Love one another, as I have loved you." We love our neighbor when, like Jesus, and the Saints, we make sacrifices for others.

❦

JUNE 23

St. Audrey (or Etheldreda)

St. Audrey was born in England. Her three sisters are also saints. She wanted to be a bride of Christ, but her parents wanted her to marry. Although she gave in to their wishes, she and her husband lived together as brother and sister. Three years later, he died, and Audrey went to live a quiet life of prayer on the island he had given her.

After five years, the Saint's relatives demanded that she marry again, and once more, Audrey gave in. Her second husband was young, and they, too, lived as brother and sister. Audrey spent all her time doing works of mercy. However, when her husband became older and was a powerful king, he wanted her to live as a wife and a queen. She replied that she belonged only to God. He tried hard to make her change her mind, but in the end, he let her become a nun.

Back on her own island again, St. Audrey founded a convent and was a very holy superior. Instead of wearing the linen clothes worn by other noble women, she chose rough wool robes for herself. She slept only a few hours and prayed the rest of the night. St. Audrey died at the exact time she said she would, and her body was put into a plain wooden coffin, as she had wanted.

Let us admire this Saint who could have enjoyed all the pleasures of the world and instead gave them all up to make sure she would gain the pleasures of Heaven.

St. John the Baptist

John's parents were Zachary and Elizabeth. Elizabeth was a cousin of Mary, the Mother of Jesus. Mary went to visit and help when Elizabeth was old and about to become a mother. When they met, Jesus Who was within Mary, sanctified John, who was not yet born.

At the birth of St. John, his father gave him the name John, as the angel had commanded. John's mission was to prepare the way for the coming of Jesus. So when he was still a young boy he went into the desert to prepare himself with silence, prayer and penance. Soon crowds started to come to him. He warned them to be sorry for their sins, and to change their lives, and he gave them the baptism of repentance. One day, Our Lord Himself came. He wanted to be baptized by St. John to begin making reparation for our sins. On that day, John

St. John the Baptist

said to his disciples that Jesus was the Messias for whom they had been waiting. He told them and everyone else to follow Him.

Later on, St. John learned that King Herod had married a woman who already had a husband and a daughter. This king was the son of the King Herod who had murdered all those little boys in Bethlehem. St. John told him that it was wrong for him to live with that woman. For this, he was put in prison. He remained a prisoner until Herod had his head cut off to please the daughter of his sinful wife.

St. John's motto was, "Jesus must become more and more, and I must become less and less."

We must remember that God is everything and we are nothing. Let us learn from St. John not to look for praise and admiration, but to do everything for the glory of God.

࿇

June 25

St. William of Monte Vergine

William was born in Northern Italy and was brought up by relatives because his parents died when he was a baby. When William grew up, he became a hermit, but when he worked a miracle and cured a blind man, he became famous. He was too humble to be pleased with the people's admiration, so he went away to live alone on a very high, wild mountain.

Even there, however, men gathered around the Saint and he built a monastery for them dedicated to the Blessed Virgin. People gave the mountain a new name now—the Mountain of the Virgin—because of William's monastery.

Later the Saint founded other great monasteries, helped by King Roger of Naples. His good influence on this king angered some evil men of the court, and they tried to show that William was really an evil man hiding behind a holy habit. They sent a bad woman to tempt him to sin. As soon as William realized what kind of a woman his visitor was, he worked a miracle and the evil woman ran away frightened.

When we are tempted to commit a sin of impurity, we should remember that after that sin we might die and go to hell to suffer forever.

June 26

St. Pelagius

This boy martyr of Spain lived in the days when the Moors ruled part of his homeland and were fighting the Spanish Christians. Pelagius was only ten when his uncle had to leave him as a hostage with the Moors in the city of Cordova. He would not be allowed to go free until his uncle sent what the Moors demanded.

Three years passed and still the young Christian remained a prisoner. By this time, he was a handsome, lively boy of thirteen, and although many of the other prisoners were men of evil habits, Pelagius was not led to sin by their example. For one so young, he had a strong will and knew how to keep himself good—even in a prison.

The ruler of the Moors heard about the handsome young prisoner and he sent for him. He liked what he saw, and he offered Pelagius his freedom, plus fine clothes to wear, beautiful horses to ride, honor, money—as long as he would give up his Faith and become a Mohammedan like his captors.

"All those things you named mean nothing to me," answered the boy firmly. "I have been a Christian. I am a Christian now. I shall continue to be a Christian." Then the ruler tried threatening Pelagius, but neither his promises nor his threats had any effect.

What courage and generosity in this young boy of thirteen! He died a martyr for his Faith. Let us ask ourselves how faithful we are at least to the few little practices of piety our Religion requires of us.

❧

June 27

Blessed Madeleine Fontaine and Her Three Companions

These four French martyrs were Sisters of Charity of St. Vincent de Paul. Besides Blessed Madeleine, there were Blessed Frances Lanel, Blessed Teresa Fantou, and Blessed Joan Gerard. They were put to death for their Faith in the bloodiest days of the French Revolution.

First, the four Sisters were arrested because they refused to take an oath that could not be taken without committing a sin. The enemies of the Church said that they had found certain papers in the convent which showed that the Sisters had been working against the Revolution. None of this was true, but a wicked judge in the city of Cambrai had Blessed Madeleine, the Superior, condemned to death, together with her three Sisters.

The Sisters walked to their execution calmly singing a hymn to the Blessed Mother, "Hail, Star of the Sea." Sister Madeleine was the last to die. As she came near the guillotine, she cried to the watching crowd: "Listen, Christians! We are the last victims. The persecution is going to stop. The altars of Jesus will rise again in glory!"

Her prophecy came true. The evil man who had judged the martyrs had to stop the executions because people were so angry with him. Six weeks later, he himself was beheaded.

No matter what happens, we should never promise to do something which is forbidden by God's law.

JUNE 28

St. Irenaeus

Irenaeus was a Greek who was born less than a hundred years after Our Lord died. He had the great privilege of being taught by St. Polycarp, who had been a disciple of St. John the Apostle. Irenaeus once told a friend: "I listened to St. Polycarp's instructions very carefully, and I wrote down his actions and his words—not on paper, but on my heart."

After he became a priest, Irenaeus was sent to the French city of Lyons. It was in this city that the Bishop, St. Pothinus, was martyred with a great many other Saints. Irenaeus missed being martyred because he was asked by his brother priests to take an important message from them to the Pope in Rome. In that letter they spoke of Irenaeus as a man full of zeal for the Faith.

When Irenaeus returned to be the Bishop of Lyons, the persecution was over. But there was another danger: a heresy called Gnosticism. This false religion attracted some people by its promise to teach them secret mysteries. Irenaeus studied all its teachings and then in five books showed how wrong they were. He wrote with politeness, because he wanted to win people for Jesus, but sometimes his words were strong, such as when he said: "As soon as a man has been won over to the Gnostics, he becomes puffed up with conceit, and self-importance, and with the majestic air of a cock, he goes strutting about." St. Irenaeus' books were read by so many people that before too long, the whole heresy began to die out.

St. Irenaeus always remembered what he had been taught by St. Polycarp. We, too, should try to forget whatever evil impressed us, and think, instead, about the good things we have heard or read. If we think well, we will live well.

JUNE 29

St. Peter

Peter, the first Pope and the prince of the Apostles, was a fisherman when Jesus invited him to follow Him, saying: "I will make you a fisher of men." Peter was a simple man who sometimes acted without thinking, but he was generous, honest and very much attached to Our Lord.

This great Apostle's name was Simon, but Jesus Himself changed it to Peter, which means "rock." "You are Peter," Jesus said, "and on this rock I shall build my Church."

Because he did not pray for strength, he became afraid when Our Lord was arrested. It was then that he committed the sin of denying Our Lord three times, but he repented, and wept over his sin the rest of his life. Jesus forgave Peter and, after His Resurrection, asked him three times: "Do you love Me?" Poor Peter! "Lord," he said, "You know all things. You know I love You." Then Our Lord said: "Feed My lambs and My sheep." He was telling Peter to rule over the whole Church, and after Our Lord went back to Heaven, Peter was the leader of all the Christians.

He went to Rome to live and converted many pagans. When a great persecution began, the Christians begged St. Peter to leave Rome and save himself. He started out, but on the road, he met Our Lord coming in. "Lord, where are You going?" Peter

St. Peter

asked. And Jesus answered, "I am coming to be crucified a second time." Then St. Peter turned around and went back, for he knew that the vision meant he was the one who was to die on the cross. He was taken prisoner and condemned to death by crucifixion. St. Peter asked to be crucified with his head downward, because he said he was not worthy to suffer as Jesus had.

If we have fallen into sin, we should not get discouraged. We should imitate St. Peter by being sorry and loving Jesus more than ever before.

❦

JUNE 30

The Martyrdom of St. Paul

St. Paul is the great Apostle who first persecuted the Christians and then was converted. At the time of his conversion, Jesus had said: "I will show him how much he must suffer for Me."

St. Paul loved Jesus Crucified very much—so much that he became a living copy of Our Divine Savior. All his life, during his many missionary trips, St. Paul met troubles and went through dangers of every kind. He was whipped, stoned, shipwrecked, and lost at sea. Many, many times, he was hungry, thirsty, and cold.

Yet, he always trusted in God. He never stopped preaching. "The love of Jesus presses me onward," he said. In reward, God gave him great comfort and joy in every suffering.

St. Paul

When St. Paul found out that the Emperor Nero had begun a terrible persecution in Rome, he hurried back to Rome to comfort and encourage the Christians. The thought of the danger did not stop him. Before long, however, he and St. Peter were also put in prison and condemned. They were led out to execution together. As they walked along, these two great heroes of Christ encouraged each other.

At a certain point they were separated. St. Peter was crucified on Vatican Hill, and St. Paul was taken and beheaded near the place where his Basilica now stands. With what faith St. Paul bowed his head to accept the blow! From prison he had written: "Behold, the time of my deliverance is at hand. I have fought the good fight. I have kept the Faith. And there is laid up for me a crown, which the Lord will give to me and to all those who love and serve Him."

When we have some trouble or little cross, let us think of St. Paul, and let us pray to him for patience and more love of God.

Alphabetical Listing
of the Saints for Volume One

Daughters of St. Paul

MASSACHUSETTS
 50 St. Paul's Ave., Jamaica Plain, Boston, MA 02130; **617-522-8911.**
 172 Tremont Street, Boston, MA 02111; **617-426-5464; 617-426-4230.**
NEW YORK
 78 Fort Place, Staten Island, NY 10301; **212-447-5071; 212-447-5086.**
 59 East 43rd Street, New York, NY 10017; **212-986-7580.**
 625 East 187th Street, Bronx, NY 10458; **212-584-0440.**
 525 Main Street, Buffalo, NY 14203; **716-847-6044.**
NEW JERSEY
 Hudson Mall—Route 440 and Communipaw Ave.,
  Jersey City, NJ 07304; **201-433-7740.**
CONNECTICUT
 202 Fairfield Ave., Bridgeport, CT 06604; **203-335-9913.**
OHIO
 2105 Ontario Street (at Prospect Ave.), Cleveland, OH 44115;
  216-621-9427.
 616 Walnut Street, Cincinnati, OH 45202; **513-721-4838; 513-421-5733.**
PENNSYLVANIA
 1719 Chestnut Street, Philadelphia, PA 19103; **215-569-2638;**
  215-864-0991
VIRGINIA
 1025 King Street, Alexandria, VA 22314; **703-683-1741; 703-549-3806.**
SOUTH CAROLINA
 243 King Street, Charleston, SC 29401.
FLORIDA
 2700 Biscayne Blvd., Miami, FL 33137; **305-573-1618; 305-573-1624.**
LOUISIANA
 4403 Veterans Memorial Blvd., Metairie, LA 70006; **504-887-7631;**
  504-887-0113.
 423 Main Street, Baton Rouge, LA 70802; **504-343-4057; 504-381-9485.**
MISSOURI
 1001 Pine Street (at North 10th), St. Louis, MO 63101; **314-621-0346;**
  314-231-1034.
ILLINOIS
 172 North Michigan Ave., Chicago, IL 60601; **312-346-4228; 312-346-3240.**
TEXAS
 114 Main Plaza, San Antonio, TX 78205; **512-224-8101; 512-224-0938.**
CALIFORNIA
 1570 Fifth Ave., San Diego, CA 92101; **619-232-1442.**
 46 Geary Street, San Francisco, CA 94108; **415-781-5180.**
WASHINGTON
 2301 Second Ave., Seattle, WA 98121; **206-623-1320; 206-623-2234.**
HAWAII
 1143 Bishop Street, Honolulu, HI 96813; **808-521-2731.**
ALASKA
 750 West 5th Ave., Anchorage, AK 99501; **907-272-8183.**

CANADA
 3022 Dufferin Street, Toronto 395, Ontario, Canada.